PHILIP LARKIN AND ENGLISH POETRY

PHILIP LARKIN AND ENGLISH POETRY

Terry Whalen

University of British Columbia Press
Vancouver   1986

International Standard Book Number 0–7748–0232–4

Printed in Hong Kong

This book has been published with the help of a grant from the Canadian Federation for the Humanities, using funds provided by the Social Sciences and Humanities Research Council of Canada.

For Maryann and my parents

Contents

Acknowledgements

Many people have helped me in the writing of this book, either by discussing particular problems with me or by encouraging me to continue my work when the going got rough. I should like to thank, particularly, R. G. Collins for his continuous and stable criticism, and his encouragement of my efforts. In addition, I thank Laurie Clancy, Bruce Martin, Jarold Ramsey, John Reibetanz and Rosemary Sullivan, all of whom have given me goodwill and good advice at various stages in the development of this study. For their editorial patience, efficiency and hard work I wish to thank Julia Steward, Frances Arnold, Valery Rose, Jane Fredeman, and Graham Eyre.

In sometimes very different versions, parts of this study have appeared in a series of magazines and journals in the form of articles and review articles I have written on Larkin over the past ten years or so. In a sense, what the reader will experience between the covers of this book is the product of a lengthy process of transformation of these earlier comments into a larger statement of literary appreciation. The advice and encouragement I have received from the editors and assessors of those journals have been of great assistance to me in the discovery of a shape for the present study. I therefore wish to thank those editors not only for permission to reprint parts of the articles here, but also for their comments and suggestions along the way. They are the editors of the *Australian Book Review*, the *Critical Quarterly*, the *Critical Review*, *Modernist Studies*, *Sift* and *Thalia: Studies in Literary Humor*.

The author and publishers wish to thank the following who have kindly given permission to quote from copyright material:

Faber & Faber Ltd and Farrar, Straus & Giroux Inc., for the extracts from Thom Gunn's *Moly* and *Jack Straw's Castle*. Faber &

Faber Ltd for the extracts from Thom Gunn's *The Sense of Movement* and *Poems 1950–1966: A Selection.*

Faber & Faber Ltd for the extracts from Philip Larkin's *The North Ship* and *The Whitsun Weddings.* Faber & Faber Ltd and Farrar, Straus & Giroux Inc., for the extracts from *High Windows.*

Harper & Row, Publishers Inc., for the extracts from Ted Hughes's *Selected Poems 1957–1967* and *Crow.*

Grafton Books, a Division of the Collins Publishing Group, for the extracts from R. S. Thomas's *Poetry for Supper, Pietà* and *Song at the Year's Turning.*

Macmillan London Ltd, for the extracts from R. S. Thomas's *H'm* and *R. S. Thomas, Later Poems, 1972–1982.*

The Marvell Press, for the extracts from Philip Larkin's *The Less Deceived.*

Viking Penguin Inc., Laurence Pollinger Ltd, and the Estate of Mrs Frieda Lawrence Ravagli, for the extracts from *The Complete Poems of D. H. Lawrence.*

Abbreviations

Page references to Larkin's main verse collections are given in the text, using the following abbreviations:

HW *High Windows* (London: Faber & Faber, 1974)
LD *The Less Deceived* (1955; repr. Hessle: Marvell Press, 1966)
NS *The North Ship* (1945; repr. with intro., London: Faber & Faber, 1966)
WW *The Whitsun Weddings* (London: Faber & Faber, 1964)

1 Introduction

In the time between his fiftieth birthday and his death in 1985, Philip Larkin's reputation has ascended to the point where even his detractors are now naming him a major poet. There are nine extensive critical and/or scholarly publications related to his achievement and they are all products of approximately the past ten years.[1] Larkin has earned a respectable critical acclaim for his novels, *Jill* (1946) and *A Girl in Winter* (1947), but it is as a poet of candour and brilliant craftsmanship that he has assured his high stature as a contemporary writer. Beyond critical recognition, the esteem in which he is held by other poets shows in the public praise accorded to him by them, and by such honours as his commission to edit *The Oxford Book of Twentieth-Century Verse* (1973).[2] This latter trust, we recall, was last given to William Butler Yeats.

Larkin's scope as a reviewer and literary commentator has recently been made visible by *Required Writing* (1983),[3] and by the publication of B. C. Bloomfield's *Philip Larkin: A Bibliography, 1933–1976* in 1979. Clive James, in *Larkin at Sixty* (1982), appreciates the poet's achievement as a critic – and, in one sense, as a poet – when he says of Larkin's criticism that it

> appeals so directly to the ear that he puts himself in danger of being thought trivial, especially by the mock-academic. Like Amis's, Larkin's readability seems so effortless that it tends to be thought of as something separate from his intelligence. But readability *is* intelligence. The vividness of Larkin's critical style is not just a token of his seriousness but the embodiment of it.[4]

It is because I agree with this appraisal of Larkin's talent as a readable critic that I have made liberal use of his own criticism in this study. There is a helpful way in which Larkin's own remarks on literature and art irradiate his own practice, and many of his

1

commentaries dispel standard misunderstandings about the kind of poetry he writes.

Philip Larkin and English Poetry is primarily a practical criticism exploration of Larkin's poetry, and a reassessment of Larkin's aesthetic and his place in the traditions of English poetry. During a lecture given at Oxford on 12 March 1975, John Wain, after a close analysis of Larkin's 'How Distant', felt compelled to add, 'I apologise for the ponderous shredding out of this beautifully lucid poem; my excuse must be the monumental thick-headedness with which Larkin's poetry is often approached: there is no explanation, however otiose, that is not needed by somebody.'[5] I quote Wain because I wish to borrow his implicit sanction in this context. There has been so much misunderstanding about Larkin's poems, and also about their cumulative effects, that a critical work which takes as its central strategy a close reading of the poetry would seem to be in order. Those who are aware of my critical essays on Larkin in the *Critical Quarterly*, the *Critical Review*, *Modernist Studies* and *Thalia* will see that I have revised and added to these essays in a way which deals with the individual poems in more detail. Each of those essays insisted that Larkin is a more complicated personality, a more explorative poet and also a more positive poet than much critical response to his work has been willing to recognise.

If we do not count Larkin's *XX Poems* (1951), which was published in a limited edition of 100 copies, he has four volumes of poetry in public view. They include *The North Ship* (1945), *The Less Deceived* (1955), *The Whitsun Weddings* (1964) and *High Windows* (1974). It is standard practice to view Larkin as a poet who develops away from what Roger Bowen has referred to as the 'self-conscious lyricism'[6] of *The North Ship* to a more mature, 'spare tone' in *The Less Deceived*, a tone which is then sustained in the volumes which follow. The growth of Larkin's sensibility, his development as a poet, is also seen as having to do with a movement away from the influence of Yeats and towards discipleship under Hardy. This shift is viewed by both Larkin's critics and the poet himself as the discarding of an early romantic impulse for the sake of a more tough-minded maturity. When *The North Ship* was reprinted in 1966, it contained an Introduction in which Larkin claimed his new freedom under Hardy's influence, and referred to the early influence of Yeats with a sense of embarrassment. Larkin noted that the 'predominance of Yeats in this volume deserves some explanation', and told how Vernon Watkins visited 'the English Club' in Oxford in 1943 and 'swamped us with Yeats'. Larkin was impressed and enthusiastic, and

> As a result I spent the next three years trying to write like Yeats, not because I liked his personality or understood his ideas but out of infatuation with his music (to use the word I think Vernon used). In fairness to myself it must be admitted that it is a particularly potent music, as pervasive as garlic, and has ruined many a better talent.

He included in the reprint an additional poem, one from *XX Poems* entitled 'Waiting for breakfast', which, he said, he had added as a 'coda' and which 'shows the Celtic fever abated and the patient sleeping soundly' (*NS*, pp. 9–10). And indeed the comment is accurate. The first stanza reads like a pastiche of early T. S. Eliot:

> Waiting for breakfast, while she brushed her hair,
> I looked down at the empty hotel yard
> Once meant for coaches. Cobblestones were wet,
> But sent no light back to the loaded sky,
> Sunk as it was with mist down to the roofs.
> Drainpipes and fire-escape climbed up
> Past rooms still burning their electric light:
> I thought: Featureless morning, featureless night.

> (*NS*, p. 48)

In its sharp immediacy, made the more precise by its function as an objective correlative, the poem is radically different from the characteristic poem xxiv of *The North Ship*, where the 'Celtic fever' Larkin refers to is running high:

> Love, we must part now; do not let it be
> Calamitous and bitter. In the past
> There has been too much moonlight and self-pity:
> Let us have done with it: for now at last
> Never has sun more boldly paced the sky,
> Never were hearts more eager to be free,
> To kick down worlds, lash forests; you and I

No longer hold them; we are husks, that see
The grain going forward to a different use.

There is regret. Always, there is regret.
But it is better that our lives unloose,
As two tall ships, wind-mastered, wet with light,
Break from an estuary with their courses set,
And waving part, and waving drop from sight.

(*NS*, p. 37)

The major difference between the two poems lies in the strength:
witness the more visual–concrete realism of the later 'Waiting for
breakfast'. Long after Larkin came to the example of Hardy's
poetry he was to claim,

> When I came to Hardy it was with the sense of relief that I
> didn't have to jack myself up to a concept of poetry that lay
> outside my own life – this is perhaps what I felt Yeats was trying
> to make me do. One could simply relapse back into one's own
> life and write from it.[7]

Larkin coincidentally gives us a broad distinction between the two
poems just quoted. Poem xxiv appears to have been given birth
out of a 'concept of poetry', a dated conviction that the 'poetic'
requires the infinitely sad theme registered in the language of
precious romantic refrain. It is a poem, therefore, which is held
together by cliché form rather than felt experience. 'Waiting for
breakfast', on the other hand, while perhaps lacking in thematic
vigour on first glance, is crafted in such a way that the feeling
expressed is more individual. A measure of the individuality of the
feeling is there in the realistic quality of its setting and in the
outward curiosity of the speaker. 'Waiting for breakfast' is,
theoretically, a more mature and 'less deceived' poem.

Larkin is undeniably a 'less deceived' poet after *The North Ship*,
but there is a tension that is written into his mature volumes,
between his new energies as an ironic poet and his concern with
beauty that is not eradicated by his new maturity. 'Waiting for
Breakfast' exists as Larkin's reassessment of his earlier 'fever', but
it also contains a sense of surprise at the passing beauty of the new
day, and an ability to question his newly found 'spare tone' as

well. Its middle stanza includes a beauty and a note of pleasure which are commonly overlooked by readers who take the poet's 'less deceived' identity at face value:

> I thought: Featureless morning, featureless night.
>
> Misjudgement: for the stones slept, and the mist
> Wandered absolvingly past all it touched,
> Yet hung like a stayed breath; the lights burnt on,
> Pin-points of undisturbed excitement; beyond the glass
> The colourless vial of day painlessly spilled
> My world back after a year, my lost lost world
> Like a cropping deer strayed near my path again,
> Bewaring the mind's last clutch. Turning, I kissed her,
> Easily for sheer joy tipping the balance to love.
>
> (*NS*, p. 48)

The operative word here, and in many of Larkin's poems, is 'misjudgement', for Larkin's 'less deceived' poetry is as likely to find that its speakers have misjudged the adequacy of their scepticism as that they must highly qualify their romantic urges. If only for a moment, there is a recovered joy in 'Waiting for breakfast', and it rises inevitably in the above lines as a sensitivity to beauty and an openness to empirical surprise.

The most unhelpful critical reaction to Larkin's move from an early romantic impulse to a 'less deceived' maturity has been a tendency amongst critics to overstate the pendulum's swing. More recent responses – and the analyses by J. R. Watson, Andrew Motion and Seamus Heaney particularly – have begun to take notice of Larkin's sensitivity to beauty; and the persistence of that openness in his volumes, I would suggest, represents an 'other' Larkin which makes him a more complicated and positive writer than has yet been appreciated in full measure.[8]

While Larkin has invoked Oscar Wilde on the matter of his development as a poet ('Oscar Wilde said that only mediocrities develop. I just don't know. I don't think I want to change; just to become better at what I am'[9]), his three major volumes show, in their design, a tendency to reach after the more positive vision, even if that reaching is also punctuated heavily with many sad, bleak, sceptical and 'less deceived' poems. Many would claim that

Larkin grows more pessimistic as he ages, and a chronological selection of poems can be made which would support that judgement. If we select such poems as 'Ambulances', 'The Building' and 'Aubade' as the makings of the case, each of these works presents us with eminently quotable lines, eminently bleak ones. On the other hand, if the selection includes instead 'Wedding Wind', 'To the Sea' and 'The Explosion', there is data for the judgement that the poet grows more optimistic as he proceeds. In short, how does one find grounds for any judgement at all? I think one should take notice of the overall design of the poet's volumes. Larkin's own identification of important triptychs in the volumes is very suggestive in this regard.

The design of *The Less Deceived*, for instance, is a relatively bleak one when judged by its central triptych of poems. The inclusion of such poems as 'Wedding Wind', 'Born Yesterday' and 'Church Going' gives the collection powerful moments of beauty. Nevertheless, the controlling triptych is a relatively disenchanted one. The volume opens with the sensation of human transience which is so central to 'Lines on a Young Lady's Photograph Album', and takes its title from a poem on rape and defeat, 'Deceptions'. And it closes with the calm but saddened lines of 'At Grass', a poem about old age. So, compelling as these importantly located poems are on their own ground, they certainly help to abet the notion that Larkin is a poet of failure and disenchantment. But the major error in criticism of Larkin's work has, I think, been the tendency of critics and reviewers to take this single volume as very strictly paridigmatic of the poet's entire achievement to date.

The Whitsun Weddings appears carefully designed as a slightly more buoyant volume than its two predecessors. It contains representatively dark poems such as 'Mr Bleaney', 'Ambulances' and 'Afternoons'. But its central triptych contains poems of beauty which would seem to locate the more 'neutral' poems to the back of volume's design. *The Whitsun Weddings* opens with 'Here', a poem which finishes on a mystical note of peace. The volume takes its title from a poem which celebrates the ordinary beauty of a ritual community event, and it closes with 'An Arundel Tomb', a piece in which the 'almost-instinct almost true' concern is that 'What will survive of us is love' (*WW*, p. 46). The triptych is dominantly a positive one, at least in terms of the poet's choice of the poems he wishes to highlight. And, in terms of Larkin's development of vision, the volume is pivotal in that it demonstrates his desire to reach after the values of beauty as much as possible, while also maintaining, on the evidence of the darker poems, his unillusioned purchase on reality.

High Windows is similarly positive in design. It opens with the celebratory witness of 'To the Sea' and takes its title from a poem which moves from cynical detachment to lines which share with earlier poems such as 'Here' a mystical intensity. *High Windows* closes with 'The Explosion', a poem which manages to move from an ironic mining-disaster to a vision of transcendence which makes it one of the most compelling religious poems of our day. While there are also frankly bleak poems in the volume, such as 'The Building', 'This be the Verse' and 'Going, Going', the major triptych is one which highly qualifies the neighbouring gloom of the darker poems. There is an obvious struggle on the poet's part to transcend, without being glib, his own habit of attention to the bleaker aspects of human experience. And he has given evidence of this will toward further meaning in the design of his last two volumes. When commentators seize on Larkin's latest effort, 'Aubade', and name it representative of his work as a whole, they exaggerate the relative weight of its gloom. It *is* a bleak poem, and we can not doubt this. Yet is is in keeping with that major cluster of poems in Larkin's canon which are impatient with meaninglessness and hungry for that which can satisfy the existential imagination. In its Hamlet-of-the-suburbs melancholy and dark whimsy, it calls 'Nothing to be Said', 'Ignorance' and 'Days' to mind. Since no individual poem or cluster of poems can safely be said to house Larkin's complete view, 'Aubade' should, I think, be recognised for what it is: a continuation of the dialectic in Larkin's writing between the bleakness and the beauty which, together, comprise his total view. In short, on the external evidence of the matter, we can at least assert that Larkin is a more explorative and open poet than first thoughts might suggest.

And this is not to assert that we should judge the achievement of Larkin – or any other poet, for that matter – by the degree to which he writes in a positive light. While a strictly depressed or strictly atoned vision might, in some instances, give evidence of a narrowness of view and a simplicity of thought, the relative cheerfulness of the vision tells us, after all, very little about the quality of the writing or the trustworthiness of that vision. Larkin is a poet whose range of vision is wider than many have perceived; and to state this at the outset is merely to start with the conventional wisdom about his dreariness placed in its proper perspective. A great deal of his achievement as a poet has to do with the strenuous pessimism of his vision, and also has to do with his struggle to go past that pessimism to a statement of the value of beauty. In the end, it is extremely difficult for the critic to measure the poet's final view – and I have only brought out the issue of the design of his volumes as a way of up-ending the method of extracting from three or four bleak poems, or a single poem, a complete view and naming it the poet's controlling one.

Larkin has undeniably shifted to a more unillusioned perspective since *The North Ship*, and his affinities with Thomas Hardy, and with the Movement writers, have had an effect on his vision and craft in this change. In the following pages I have tried to add to this view a recognition that he also shares central affinities with other writers who are 'less deceived' (Dr Johnson, most centrally), or who have managed to sustain a qualified romanticism in their visions almost in spite of their knowledge of innumerable reasons for despair. It is in this regard that the examples of the Imagists and of D. H. Lawrence are important, I think – important in a way which should up-end all pat and easy commentary on Larkin's dreariness as a poet.

Larkin's achievement is amenable to discussion next to many more poets than I have examined in this study, and it is worth saying in passing that Thomas Hardy, William Butler Yeats, W. H. Auden and Louis MacNeice are figures who come to mind as influences whose effects on Larkin are likely continually to be noticed and detailed by future critics.[10] I have kept my own commentary closer to the affinities Larkin shares with Johnson, the Imagists and Lawrence because it is in the region of these specific influences that I have found not only overlooked likenesses, but the shapes of craft and vision which seem to me most centrally to mark off the finer details of his achievement. In addition, I have avoided in-depth study of Larkin's affinities with the Movement writers, and with an almost endless series of living poets who share with him related craft and thematic concerns. Instead of listing, piecemeal, affinities he has with many contemporaries, I have drawn attention to only a core of living British poets who share with Larkin a profound legacy from the example of D. H. Lawrence and the Imagists. While Larkin's relationship to the Movement writers has had an effect on his work, it has always seemed to me that his proper contemporary peers are poets such as Ted Hughes, Thom Gunn and R. S. Thomas – poets who not only are closest to him in the depth and integrity of their craftsmanship, but also share with him a rediscovered value in a strategy of wondrous observation. As poets of reality, all these writers have valued, along with Larkin, an outwardly witnessing poetry which goes past subjectivism in its struggle toward a healing connection with surrounding life. As poets of profound doubts, tensions and existentional anxieties, theirs is a shared exploration which is everywhere attentive to the bleaker truths and realities of our day. Nevertheless, it is in their persistent search for meaning in the external world that the human spirit can be said to assert itself with a fresh curiosity after the almost terminal despair of much of the wasteland writing of the century.

To some readers, the contexts and affinities in which I have placed Larkin might initially seem unusual and improper in a practical criticism of his work. So I have also designed the structure of this study in a manner which deals with customary reference points in Larkin criticism – reference points such as the nature of his poetic personality; his 'less deceived' identity as a poet; his achievement as a nature poet; his concerns as a poet of the commonplace; and the experiential nature of his aesthetic of poetry. In all of this, of course, I have aimed for the effect sought after by most appreciative works of literary criticism. I have attempted to state my understanding of the poetry in a way which will encourage new readers to recognise the complexity of the poet's art, and at the same time return seasoned readers to the poetry with additional reasons for their praise and for consent to the poet's major status.

Note added in proof
Philip Larkin's death in 1985 occurred just as this study was going to press. It is with a feeling of loss, esteem and further regard that *Philip Larkin and English Poetry* is therefore now also dedicated to the memory of the poet.

2   Poetic Personality

Larkin has said of the poem 'Absences', 'I fancy it sounds like a different, better poet rather than myself',[1] and, when Ian Hamilton proposed to him that 'Church Going' reads like a 'debate between a poet and a *persona*', the poet agreed and said that it is 'seeking an answer. I suppose that's the antithesis you mean. I think one has to dramatize oneself a little.'[2] On another occasion he said, 'What I should like to write is different kinds of poems that might be by different people. Someone once said that the great thing is not to be different from other people, but to be different from yourself.'[3] There are many 'different people' in Larkin's volumes to date. Hardyesque fatalists, Swiftian cynics, Audenesque blasphemers, Yeatsian bards and Betjemanesque local historians – to cite familiar voices – compete for attention in his works.

Larkin alters his tone and posture within poems; and he alters his ground tone from one poem to the next. These facts, and the poet's comments on his desire to find the voice of a better self, serve notice of impending trouble for critics who seek to discover a single disposition of personality in his volumes: his poetic personality is a dramatic one above all. Larkin admits to a tendency toward gloominess in his work ('If I'd been a different person and different things had happened to me, I might have written differently'[4]), but he self-consciously reacts to the limits of his established personality, and the result is poetry which moves continually in the direction of self-criticism and altered attitudes to experience.

Larkin is a dramatic poet in the sense that he creates centres of consciousness which are not necessarily expressive of his entire view, but are created, rather, as personae which liberate the poet to explore the multiple concerns of his art. Bruce Martin speaks for many critics when he says that the poetry 'suggests a marked identity between speaker and poem', and the poet 'projects a sincerity and forthrightness by which he unwittingly invites

10

speculation about himself'.[5] The 'true voice of human feeling' is unmistakably there in his poems. But it is a complicated voice indeed, and the sometimes-startling difference between any two Larkin poems shows that he employs different postures habitually. The wondrous reverie of the bride in 'Wedding Wind', for instance, is so different from the black humour and pessimism central to the persona in 'Aubade' that, in the narrowest of senses, it is hard to conceive of either poem as written by the same poet who mocks his way through 'Days' or 'Poetry of Departures'.

Many of Larkin's personae are humorous and sarcastic, while others are sad (with varying shades of sensitivity), and yet others are governed by an impulse to praise, have a regard for beauty and a hunger for mystical experience. There are many Larkins, and they blend and compete with one another more than the customary generalities about the poet's personality suggest. So I divide them only temporarily, and for the sake of argument, as a way of freeing them from the homogeneity that criticism of Larkin's work tends to favour in the name of finding the essential Larkin groundtone. Larkin is a poet who can be said to have a residual tone to his work, I think, but it is something as wide as a creative and self-critical scepticism rather than a simple quality of sarcasm, boredom, bleakness, sadness or sentimentality – to use just some of the labels which appear in the commentary on his work to date.

A few of Larkin's speakers are sarcastic and ostensibly very smug in their postures, and that fact has gained for him, especially amongst critics who favour viewing him as a Movement poet, a reputation for tonal fecklessness and even a twisted will. Many of his critics have claimed that he is sarcastic, sardonic, vicious, mean-minded and crass in his attempts at wit, but not really amusing after all. If one thinks the critics are themselves being vicious in making such claims, one should recall 'The Life with a Hole in It' and step far back from the blast as the poet scorns the two kinds of writer he is not, the two kinds of writer he dislikes:

> So the shit in the shuttered château
> Who does his five hundred words
> Then parts out the rest of the day
> Between bathing and booze and birds
> Is far off as ever, but so

> Is that spectacled schoolteaching sod
> (Six kids, and a wife in pod,
> And her parents coming to stay). . . .[6]

Light verse? No. 'The Life with a Hole in It' comes out of a reservoir of '*Take that you bastard*' poems (the phrase is from 'Poetry of Departures', *LD*, p. 34) which has stimulated a critical record wherein some laugh, and some don't, when the poet shows himself falling, as he does above, between two fools. And the issue is perhaps the more critically disquieting given that even Larkin's advocates have expressed reservations about his tonal sarcasm. Anthony Thwaite, for example, a critic who has done a great deal to underline Larkin's gifts as a poet, declares that he gets a bit annoyed with 'what might be called the Yah-Boo side of Larkin's work – a side not often apparent, which he shares sporadically with his admired (and admiring) fellow undergraduate from St John's, Kingsley Amis'.[7] Another advocate, Patrick Swinden, says that the 'mud pies Larkin likes to throw' are perhaps just the 'price we have to pay for Larkin's getting the silliness out of his system and thereby leaving the good poems free from infection'.[8] And there is some truth in this claim. There is abundant evidence that the poet has a bizarre wit and that he simply must let loose crazily every once in a while. Once asked, for instance, what he thought of children, he replied, 'I've never lived in hideous contact with them, having toast flung about at breakfast and so on. Perhaps worse than toast.'[9] Shades of W. C. Fields? And he can be just as vicious about his own person. Asked, on one occasion, what he thought he looked like, he promptly replied, 'Like a bald salmon.'[10]

Some of Larkin's friends act this way too. Alan Bennett, one of the co-authors of *Beyond the Fringe*, announces in *Larkin at Sixty* that 'A birthday party for Philip Larkin is like treating Simone Weil to a candlelit dinner for two at a restaurant of her choice. Or sending Proust flowers' – and, even more delicately, 'Being a librarian doesn't help: I've always found them close relatives of the walking dead. Of course this book is presumably not addressed to the librarian. I imagine all librarians get at sixty is piles.'[11] Larkin's jesting, like that of his friends, is at one level (its funniest) an almost entirely bizarre posture, a toying with sarcasm for its own sake.

Nevertheless, the poet himself is quite seriously theoretical about the value of literary horseplay and he has made comments on the matter in the abstract. 'Readers find it exceedingly difficult to combine notions of being serious and being funny',[12] he remarks, and, in a note of praise for W. H. Auden, he expresses his appreciation of that poet's 'unique blend of dedication and irreverence'.[13] He observes that 'the silliness is part of the seriousness'[14] in Stevie Smith's poetry, and, in an interview with John Haffenden, quite soberly states, 'I think what survives of us is love, whether in the simple biological sense or just in terms of responding to life, making it happier, even if it's only making a joke.'[15] In the context of defining John Betjeman's flexibility of voice, he seems to suggest that Betjeman has the very tonal friskiness which he himself seeks for one of his own postures as a poet:

> Betjeman is serious: his subjects are serious, and the fact that his tone can be light or ambivalent should not deceive us into thinking he does not treat them seriously. His texture is a subtle, a constant flickering between solemn and comic, self-mockery and self expression . . . he offers us, indeed, something we cannot find in any other writer – a gaiety, a sense of the ridiculous.[16]

Larkin quite obviously prizes the 'comic', the self-mockery', the 'sense of the ridiculous' in poetry. The fact that he included Elizabeth Wordsworth's 'Good and Clever' in his edition of *The Oxford Book of Twentieth-Century Verse* (1973) evidences his respect for the ideal she holds up in that poem. It is worth recalling the charm in that poem, as Larkin seems to have drawn upon it in his own poetry:

> If all the good people were clever,
> 　And all the clever people were good,
> The world would be nicer than ever
> 　We thought that it possibly could.
> But somehow 'tis seldom or never
> 　The two hit it off as they should,
> The good are so harsh to the clever,
> 　The clever, so rude to the good!

> So, friends, let it be our endeavour
> To make each other understood;
> For few can be good, like the clever,
> Or clever, so well as the good.[17]

Larkin is both a serious and a clever poet, and, in a central comment he makes on the difficulty of orchestrating tone and attitude in poetry, he adopts Wordsworth's wisdom and goes past it to yet deeper matters. It is potentially soothing, I think, to those readers who initially find him merely sarcastic and embittered:

> The poet is perpetually in that common condition of trying to feel a thing because he believes it, or believe a thing because he feels it.
>
> Except when springing from those rich and narrow marches where the two concur, therefore, his writing veers perpetually between the goody-goody-clever-clever and the silly-shameful-self-indulgent, and there is no point in inclining towards one kind of failure rather than another. All he can do is hope that he will go on getting flashes of what seems at the time like agreement between their opposed impulses.[18]

This is quintessential Larkin; it states well, and without jargon, the struggle in his work to achieve a rare eloquence, a poise of tone and attitude which is identifiable as a sincerity, one that resists the sentimental and the simply clever at the same time.

Larkin characteristically explores the more serious subsoil of his speakers' minds in his poetry as he moves their established, often simply clever, personalities into more generous attitudes. The well-known 'Church Going', often used as evidence of his boredom with life, is an interesting and paradigmatic case in point. It creates a modulation of tone and interplay between two basic personality traits in the poet's work as a whole: the one comic or clever, the other more open and sensitive. A central reality about the figure in 'Church Going' is that his initial wryness of manner is only the established personality, the detached laziness of which is gradually recognised as inadequate to the demands of the experience. In the first stanza he is cast as obnoxiously smug, so it is easy to overlook the more serious identity that is almost successfully concealed by an ironic mask:

Once I am sure there's nothing going on
I step inside, letting the door thud shut.
Another church: matting, seats, and stone,
And little books; sprawlings of flowers, cut
For Sunday, brownish now; some brass and stuff
Up at the holy end; the small neat organ;
And a tense, musty, unignorable silence,
Brewed God knows how long. Hatless, I take off
My cycle-clips in awkward reverence.

(*LD*, p. 28)

His scepticism of manner verges on the totally cynical. His list of observations is glibly tossed off in the diction of a wry reporter. We are almost convinced – by such phrases as 'some brass and stuff / Up at the holy end' – that he is tiredly above it all, that the scene is unworthy of his attention. But, in a telling moment of off-guardedness, he takes off his cycle clips in 'awkward reverence'. It is from a recognition of what this gesture means that the poem develops. There is more to this person than an easy disposition of boredom and irony; and the poem moves forward as a discovery of what that is. On one level, that is, the poem is an exploration of the self, with the church acting as an immediately present stimulus, an agitant which chips away at the speaker's ironic cleverness, mitigating the harshness of the initial posture. As the exploration proceeds, what we witness is the gradual ascension of a more serious voice, the emergence of a curious doubleness of identity in the speaker. Where one voice is sceptical and often turns to the caustic, the other is more sensitive and struggles toward praise. Each voice, in fact, represents one of the major impulses in Larkin's poetry: the ironic and the wondrous. The two impulses, in this case, erupt and subside, sometimes competitively, sometimes co-operatively, at every turn in the explorative psychological drama of the poem until, in the final three stanzas, the impulses are welded together into the expression of a richer, more unified sensibility than the one which displays a weary wit at the beginning of the poem. At this later point, the ironic reserve and reverence adjust and temper each other, giving a further and more mature coherence to both:

                                    I wonder who
Will be the last, the very last, to seek
This place for what it was; one of the crew
That tap and jot and know what rood-lofts were?
Some ruin-bibber, randy for antique,
Or Christmas-addict, counting on a whiff
Of gowns-and-bands and organ-pipes and myrrh?
Or will he be my representative,

Bored, uninformed, knowing the ghostly silt
Dispersed, yet tending to this cross of ground
Through suburb scrub because it held unspilt
So long and equably what since is found
Only in separation – marriage, and birth,
And death, and thoughts of these – for which was built
This special shell? For, though I've no idea
What this accoutred frowsty barn is worth,
It pleases me to stand in silence here.

A serious house on serious earth it is,
In whose blent air all our compulsions meet,
Are recognised, and robed as destinies.
And that much never can be obsolete,
Since someone will forever be surprising
A hunger in himself to be more serious,
And gravitating with it to this ground,
Which, he once heard, was proper to grow wise in,
If only that so many dead lie round.

                                    (*LD*, p. 29)

The early defensive irony is now transformed into a satirical good humour. The references to the 'ruin-bibber' and to the 'Christmas-addict' not only are evocative of absurd contemporary types, but the fact that the speaker feels pressured to mock them also shows a desire on his part to protect the sanctity of the ground. The irony and humour are no longer simply clever; both are now protective of the value of the place and ballast to the praise embodied in the last stanza.

    What throws many of Larkin's readers off is the surface effect of his irony, an effect which sometimes makes it appear that there is no 'hunger in himself to be more serious'. Indeed, it is an ostensibly bored and sardonic figure who crashes about in 'Church Going', viewing most sacred objects with ironic scorn. Yet, quite typically, by the time he finishes his investigation he is praising his surroundings with a musing that gives to his agnostic humanism an oddly religious glow. His mocking tones are most useful as a guard against pomposity. When Larkin is most strongly sarcastic, he is often moving carefully and ironically toward praise. His irony tends, therefore, to act as a device of exploration more than a shield signifying a recoil from experience. As in 'Church Going', so in many of his other poems: the speaker is curious about his surroundings and the poem curious about the speaker, the structure of the work being a strategy of discovery, a desire to find an intelligibility to the world that surrounds the speaker.

Larkin's tonal sarcasm (qualified as it appears to be) combines with a loneliness in many of his speakers and this helps to substantiate the charge that he is a more detached writer than evidence in 'Church Going' would seem to suggest. As in 'Church Going', the central figure speaking, in many instances, is either a solitary or something of an isolate. The speaker in 'Here', for example, states a preference for 'Isolate villages, where removed lives / Loneliness clarifies' (*WW*, p. 9). Additionally, in 'Vers de Société' there is the expression of a desire to stay clear of society, the 'forks and faces' of dinner parties, and spend time instead 'Under a lamp, hearing the noise of the wind, / And looking out to see the moon thinned / To an air-sharpened blade' (*HW*, p. 35). There is a distinct loner quality visible in many of his poetic characters, and this is easily confused with a kind of Prufrockian withdrawal. But solitude, in Larkin's poetry, is never expressed as a product of what Thom Gunn calls 'sitting irresolute all day at stool / Inside the heart'.[19] As in 'Church Going', solitary being does not preclude an active state of imaginative thinking, one in which the immediate world is present as observed or is never very far away as a vital concern. A more recent example, and a paradigmatic one, is 'High Windows':

> When I see a couple of kids
> And guess he's fucking her and she's
> Taking pills or wearing a diaphragm,
> I know this is paradise

Everyone old has dreamed of all their lives –
Bonds and gestures pushed to one side
Like an outdated combine harvester,
And everyone going down the long slide

To happiness, endlessly. I wonder if
Anyone looked at me, forty years back,
And thought, *That'll be the life;*
No God any more, or sweating in the dark

About hell and that, or having to hide
What you think of the priest. He
And his lot will all go down the long slide
Like free bloody birds. And immediately

Rather than words comes the thought of high windows:
The sun-comprehending glass,
And beyond it, the deep blue air, that shows
Nothing, and is nowhere, and is endless.

(*HW*, p. 17)

Larkin's work is punctuated – some would say punctured – by such sudden phrases as 'In a pig's arse, friend', 'Books are a load of crap', or '*stuff your pension!*'. Amazingly, such phrases have burned the ears of his more genteel critics, though the poet himself innocently claims, 'I don't think I've ever shocked for the sake of shocking.'[20] The opening lines of 'High Windows' are full of a now-familiar wiseacre bearing. The initial tone is that of a bored and supremely detached cynic. But the mocking tone and diction should not distract us from realising that this is another explorative poem and a conservative one in which 'fucking' is first envied but finally reassessed. There is a more serious underself to the speaker which moves past the confines of established personality and struggles toward a more expansive appreciation of what freedom can mean. The poem is an assault on the inadequacy of the glibness prized at the outset, an exploration that undercuts the initial blindness in the name of something gradually discovered as more profound.

At first glance the young people's liberation from old sexual mores is consented to in the easy colloquial tone; the matter-of-fact complacency of the acceptance of the new values is not questioned in the first stanza. As a unit of thought, the stanza has a finality about it that seems to close the case on a superficial level of judgement. The ostensibly bored commentator seems too tired, if not too lazy, to move any further than his wry gesture. But, although the stanza ends, the sentence appropriately continues. In an arabesque of stanzaic and syntactical form, it accumulates an undertone of more creative scepticism that ultimately – as the next stanzas enact the fits and starts of a mind intent on moving its way through appearance – casts the earlier tone of glib and defeatist acceptance in an ironic structure and undercuts it masterfully with a more open and wondrous musing. Not untypically, the language in the earlier stanzas is that of cynical disbelief; like the figure in 'Church Going', the speaker here supposes himself to have progressed past all of this superstition. As a result, the more mystical attitude that concludes the poem is understandably an attenuated one at best – there only in so far as he will move away from his scepticism. Yet, for all of that, it is there as the measured wonder of an agnostic, an urbanely contemporary mystic. The speaker is cautious of his vision, 'that shows / Nothing, and is nowhere'; he realises the fragility of his posture. But his mind is still open, compelled by the 'sun-comprehending glass' and by what is beyond it – the 'deep blue air' which is 'endless'. Even if the moment is qualified by the sense of its potential emptiness, it is for all of that a vision which orders his experience. The moment is one not of religious transcendence but of suggested possibilities of an imaginative freedom that encourages him beyond the 'nothing' he initially felt when he glanced jealously at the 'couple of kids'. The speaker uses his image of the high windows, 'Rather than words', to communicate his feeling that life might, or should be, more than the 'going down' into the ironic freedom that he finally sees as the fate of the young people and of himself in his younger years. Ironically, the different forms of licence were wrongly viewed as 'freedom' in the beginning; because of the rising epiphany of the last stanza, the going *'down the long slide / Like free bloody birds'* is finally understood as a mere reduction downward.

As in 'Church Going', the ironic and the more sensitive impulses are again in tandem. The sceptical viewpoint, while at first given to sarcastic glibness, becomes ultimately the agent of more serious concerns. The movement of both poems is one which carefully searches for meaning in the actual, immediately visible world, as the attention of the speaker moves away from the glib and toward the profound and connects with a primary region of his imagination. Clearly, the figure we come to know is a relatively solitary one and his first gestures are those of a withdrawn and jaded personality; but the established personality is transformed into something quite different in the end. Stated in another way, Anthony Thwaite tells us that 'Larkin once said to me that he would like to write a poem with such elaborate stanzas that one could wander round in them as in the aisles and side-chapels of some great cathedral',[21] and 'High Windows' employs that kind of stanzaic convolution to achieve its effects. In this poem, and in many of Larkin's works, the lines move expansively within the bounds of traditional, rhyming stanzas as they carry their observations of the actual world toward fresh epiphany and an eloquent closing. The close of the poem expands into a variation in its line length and ascends with cadence and imagery to a moment of contemplative song.

Larkin's surface cleverness only thinly veils the decidedly more serious dimension of his personality. Moreover, just as some of his wryness guards him against pomposity (that foolishness of a different order) in his solitary and contemplative poems, it also acts as a guard against sentimentality in his more gregarious ones, those moving outward in response to the lives of others. His early 'Born Yesterday', from the reputedly bleak *The Less Deceived*, is a typical instance in this regard. It was written on the occasion of Sally Amis's birth:

> Tightly-folded bud,
> I have wished you something
> None of the others would:
> Not the usual stuff
> About being beautiful,
> Or running off a spring
> Of innocence and love –
> They will all wish you that,
> And should it prove possible,
> Well, you're a lucky girl.
>
> But if it shouldn't, then
> May you be ordinary;

Have, like other women,
An average of talents:
Not ugly, not good-looking,
Nothing uncustomary
To pull you off your balance,
That, unworkable itself,
Stops all the rest from working.
In fact, may you be dull –
If that is what a skilled,
Vigilant, flexible,
Unemphasised, enthralled
Catching of happiness is called.

(*LD*, p. 24)

In his recent interview with John Haffenden, Larkin remarks, 'I don't understand the word sentimentality. It reminds me of Dylan Thomas's definition of an alcoholic: "A man you don't like who drinks as much as you do." I think sentimentality is someone you don't like feeling as much as you do.'[22] For all of the surface cleverness of 'Born Yesterday', Larkin is actually risking sentimentality by the very choice of his subject matter in this case. The apparent brutality of such deflating locutions as 'may you be dull' is mitigated by the feeling revealed in the magically appropriate image 'Tightly-folded bud', and in the syntactic and adjectival earnestness of the concluding lines, lines which wander earnestly upward toward praise and hope. That the speaker displays a scepticism regarding the 'usual stuff / About being beautiful' indicates an unsentimental honesty in his struggle to reach after firmer values. The poem is completed with an expression of good faith and a concern for the child that is not dependent on a twisted sense of the real world; what we see at work here is not cynicism, but an energetic and enlivened honesty to fact and feeling. Irony in the poem is both an explorative and a disciplining device, a springboard for the genuine feeling and a protection against the insult of maudlin sentimentality. Larkin once observed that Leslie Stephen 'gave Hardy his poetic credo in a sentence that is really all anyone needs to know about writing poetry'. That sentence included the directive, 'The ultimate aim of the poet should be to touch our hearts by showing his own.'[23] Those who understandably mistake Larkin's habit of irony for a

shield against the world and against feeling might be surprised
that he should even entertain such a soft notion for his own
aesthetic. But 'Born Yesterday' evidences that he not only agrees
with Stephen, but also enacts the precept in the midst of his
also-clever poems.

Nor is 'Born Yesterday' an isolated example of his capacity for
taking emotional risks. All of his volumes contain poems which
make the emotional statements of other contemporary poets seem
relatively inhibited, filtered through the mind or histrionic. In the
more recent volume *High Windows*, there is again the same
emotional strength, the same willingness to explore feelings even
next to the uglier aspects of being human. 'The Old Fools' is a case
in point. The subject of that poem provides the poet with a
challenging demand on his poetic; for, if in our response to the
newborn it is difficult to transcend sentimental cliché, our
difficulty with the aged and dying is that they frequently strike us
dumb:

> What do they think has happened, the old fools,
> To make them like this? Do they somehow suppose
> It's more grown-up when your mouth hangs open and drools,
> And you keep pissing yourself, and can't remember
> Who called this morning? Or that, if they only chose,
> They could alter things back to when they danced all night,
> Or went to their wedding, or sloped arms some September?
> Or do they fancy there's really been no change,
> And they've always behaved as if they were crippled or tight,
> Or sat through days of thin continuous dreaming
> Watching light move? If they don't (and they can't), it's
> strange:
> Why aren't they screaming?

> (*HW*, p. 19)

It is not difficult to recognise the speaker's apparent disrespect at
the beginning as so much posturing fakery. The tossed-off
smugness of the lingo is there as both a resistance and a
springboard to the reality, and to the very different feelings with
which the poem moves. The clever surface effects not only keep
the ugliness somewhat at bay, they also draw the mind gradually
toward the reality of the old people's lives. Characteristically, the

movement of sensibility progresses past the apparent brutal wryness to a more capacious tone of tough compassion and bewildered reverence, an agnostic allowance and hope, above all, that these lives have accomplished a perfection which transcends their physical debasement by time:

> Perhaps being old is having lighted rooms
> Inside your head, and people in them, acting.
> People you know, yet can't quite name; each looms
> Like a deep loss restored, from known doors turning,
> Setting down a lamp, smiling from a stair, extracting
> A known book from the shelves; or sometimes only
> The rooms themselves, chairs and a fire burning,
> The blown bush at the window, or the sun's
> Faint friendliness on the wall some lonely
> Rain-ceased midsummer evening. That is where they live:
> Not here and now, but where all happened once.
>   This is why they give
>
> An air of baffled absence, trying to be there
> Yet being here.

                                        (*HW*, pp. 19–20)

As in 'Lines on a Young Lady's Photograph Album', the poem finds a hope that time does not simply debase, but also distills. This is the only stabilising thought in the situation, and it is given life in the dance of images which make up the memories above. When earlier the speaker had asked, 'Why aren't they screaming?', we are so taken up with his sarcasm that we perhaps miss the recognition that the panic is really his own. The respect he learns for the old fools, despite his ironic gestures, is based partly on his recognition of their mysterious calm, as opposed to his own mortal fears. There is a final tenderness felt next to the aged which is entirely missed if we are waylaid by the irony of the title; were it more blandly titled 'The Young Fools' it would miss the ironic contrast between potential, aged wisdom and youthful naïveté, old poise and young panic.

Again, we recognise Larkin's dramatisation of personality as a discovery that wryness – in its raw state and on its own – is tonally inadequate to the mystery and possible beauty of existence, however tenuously grasped. 'The million-petalled flower / Of being here', coming as it does from Larkin's more open and romantic impulse as a poet, highly qualifies the terror of the uglier images and feelings which the poem seeks to transcend. The above stanza, taken on its own, is the embodiment of a potentially sentimental portrayal of life; but it is also a gathering-in of moments of felt meaning which are given validity by virtue of the more inclusive tonal ranging of the poem as a whole. Larkin does not finally resolve his qualms about mortality in this poem. He explores both the ground for terror and the reasons for hope in the situation, and leaves the reader in a state of contemplation. 'Well, / We shall find out', he concludes (*HW*, p. 20), and leaves us pondering the possibilities of meaning rather than neatly and complacently delivering us to a point of resolution into final conviction. If 'The Old Fools' concludes anything definite at all, it is a conclusion which is in the very activity of the verse as a comment on both the value of scepticism and its limitations. In its departure from the safe anchorage of the established personality, 'The Old Fools' discovers compassion for others and a contemplation which includes a feeling for mystery and beauty. The careful inconclusiveness of Larkin's more contemplative poems is a measure of his explorative nature as a poet and is a final signification that he sees the sarcasm of his established personality as being inadequate to the demands of experience.

And if, in Larkin's collections, his ironic persona often competes with – and loses to – an impulse toward praise and beauty, his posture as a poet of sadness matures by way of a directly analogous process. If his ironic persona does not simply express a revulsion from experience, neither does his sad persona merely record an emotional fatigue, even though sadness is one of his more characteristic tones. Just as there are poems in which the groundtone is one of humour or of praise, there are also many in which a basically sad tone is struck, though the instances in which that is exclusively so are rare. Along with his tone of humour and his tone of praise, sadness contributes significantly to his overall orchestration of feeling without dominating his voice. Most critics refer to Larkin's sadness in one way or another. Some judge it as signification of a passive quality in his pessimism and others view it as an immaturity in his personality, an absorption in a sort of life passivity. The objections tend, that is, to be aimed at the psychological base of the poetry, and often aim to correct him for failing to be emotionally mature. So it becomes more than a little interesting to discover that there is a thoughtful coherence in the poet's use of the tone, and it is a coherence which amounts to a rudimentary philosophy of sadness which informs a great deal of his vision as a humanist.

Larkin appreciates the emotion of sadness as the basic emotion which connects us compassionately with other human beings. For Larkin, to know sadness is to realise one's humanity and the humanity of others in the midst of a highly limited human condition, a condition which strong judgement shows to be enormously brutal. In what he says of sadness in Hardy's novels, it is obvious that he considers it one of the most important philosophical emotions and also a benchmark of our basic humanity:

> The dominant emotion in Hardy is sadness. Hardy was peculiarly well equipped to perceive the melancholy, the misfortune, the failing elements of life . . . the real critic of Hardy could, I think, develop a thesis concerning the two-fold value Hardy placed on suffering: first, he thought it was 'true' ('Tragedy is true guise, Comedy lies'); secondly, it could be demonstrated that Hardy associated sensitivity to suffering and awareness of the causes of pain with superior spiritual character.
>
> It would follow, therefore, that the presence of pain in Hardy's novels is a positive, not a negative quality – not the mechanical working out of some pre-determined allegiance to pessimism or any other concept, but the continual imaginative celebration of what is both the truest and the most important element in life, most important in the sense of most necessary to spiritual development.[24]

Much of this is pertinent to his own work. His comment, for instance, that Hardy's sadness is not the outgrowth of a 'pre-determined allegiance to pessimism' is clearly applicable, and we have already seen Larkin's capacity for striking the more positive note. Additionally, Larkin's own 'sensitivity to suffering' has become, for many of his readers, the hallmark of his work. Lolette Kuby, in her *An Uncommon Poet for the Common Man*, for example, deals at length with Larkin's 'awareness of the causes of pain'. Nevertheless, the similarity to Hardy stops there. Larkin, quite obviously, trusts the comic spirit in poetry more than did Hardy; and on the evidence of the poetry he would seem to differ from Hardy's conviction that comedy is evasive. It is because of this difference, in part, that Larkin's sadness is often free of the unalleviated, insistent quality of chagrin we find in Hardy's work. Yet, further to the specific similarities and differences between the two writers on the point, the more striking thing about Larkin's comments is that they indicate a good deal of scrutiny of the emotion, and of its relation to the writer's sensibility and his controlling perception of the human condition. In short, any examination of the critical record will show that he has examined the issue more thoroughly than his critics. It was A. E. Housman who claimed, during the years of the Great War, that it is precisely the 'essential business of poetry' to 'harmonize the sadness of the universe'.[25] Larkin works within that respected sanction for poetry, and the result is a level of seriousness in his work which blends with both his humour and his penchant for praise and beauty.

Larkin's sensitivity to the sadness of the human condition is connected with his basic view of the incompleteness, the imperfection, of it. In his view of that condition, what connects us all is the irony of the discrepancy between our spiritual wants and the designs of a world that fails to satisfy them. Just as we struggle for the harmony of fulfilment, time and death effortlessly conspire against us. This all sounds very Hardyesque, and it might partly account for what draws Larkin to Hardy's work despite the difference that Larkin's tone of sadness is alleviated by a markedly stronger perception of the more positive aspects of life. Still, as in Hardy, his work is everywhere informed with the focusing power on life that the fact of death commands. Although there is, as Frederick Grubb aptly states it, 'nothing of the grovelling before death'[26] in Larkin's work, the intransigent irony of death constantly evokes the demand for a mature sadness at the emotional core of his humanism.

If the human experience of the world is scarred by a hunger for perfection, death serves as a reminder of the futility of that desire, not the attainment of it. For Larkin, life has a sadness that flows through the world as a particularised version of Wordsworth's 'still, sad music of humanity'.[27] Wordsworth's phrase is especially suitable because it suggests a fact of life which is both outside the self and yet closely connected with one's own humanity. It is a music that Larkin has transcribed with an exceptional degree of poignancy in his work as a whole, and in 'Home is so Sad' it arrives as the most explicit subject matter of the poem:

> Home is so sad. It stays as it was left,
> Shaped to the comfort of the last to go
> As if to win them back. Instead, bereft
> Of anyone to please, it withers so,
> Having no heart to put aside the theft
>
> And turn again to what it started as,
> A joyous shot at how things ought to be,
> Long fallen wide. You can see how it was:
> Look at the pictures and the cutlery,
> The music in the piano stool. That vase.

(*WW*, p. 17)

This instance gives a special veracity to the repeated critical claim that Larkin is a poet of common humanity. 'Home is so Sad' is about ordinary humanity in a human condition in which even the daily objects of our world take on a natural symbolism which embody the deepest truths about our fate. There is nothing maudlin in its tone; if it is melancholic, it is not entirely defeatist when examined carefully. Any pessimism that is involved in its viewpoint is a strong pessimism, not a weak expression of despair. There is too much compassion and praise of small human courage in the poem for that kind of selfishness of emotion to survive. The pathos of humanity is significantly made visible in the scoriae of the objects in the home. As with the 'wear on the threshold' which the poet prizes in Hardy's poetry, the objects in the poem are revealed as speaking with a naturally symbolic effect. The selflessness of the speaker, the entirely beholding bearing of his persona, is assured by the manner in which the objects filter through his consciousness in a clarifying and highly suggestive way. He is there as witness to the human, lends us his eyes for the motion outward to the scene. The scene comes close to speaking for itself and the speaker brings the reader's humanity into close contact with an embodied abstraction which is inseparable from the visualised setting itself. The viewpoint of the persona is coloured by the viewer's disposition toward sadness, but his sensibility is coloured also by what is viewed. The essential consonance of viewer and viewed in this case catches the 'still, sad music of humanity', and also an intelligent sense of the contingency of that music on the empirical evidence of the immediate world. The sadness has both a stimulus and an objective correlative that establish its integrity.

There is also a unique quality to the sadness, one easily overlooked because of the heaviness, weightiness, we usually associate with the emotion. The essential sadness of the human condition can seem to give to it a kind of desperate beauty which is peculiarly and almost correspondingly atoning, that is, and in a less forlorn way this insight makes its presence felt within Larkin's sad persona. One notices, for example, that in the speaker's response to the 'joyous shot at how things ought to be', and in the strange quality of beauty in the objects of the home, there is a delicate but profound appreciation of human life. This registration of an ambiguous quality in life, an odd mixture of the tragic with an essential beauty, is too often overlooked in the criticism of Larkin's poetry, no doubt because his sadness of tone is commonly confused by a stock notion that sadness expresses only a despair with life and a withdrawal from experience. But in Larkin's poetry the sharp recognition of failure and death is not a signal of despair, even if the poet quite often comes close to such a form of fatigue. On more than one count he is more positive than this, and in a comment he has made about Betjeman's growing preoccupation with death he perceives a quality in the work of that poet which also belongs to his own:

> Fear of death is too much of a screaming close-up to allow the poetic faculty to function properly, but demands expression by reason of its very frightfulness. Nonetheless, it benefits his [Betjeman's] poetry, making the colours brighter and the beauties more transiently poignant by contrast, giving a seasoning of honesty and a grim sense of proportion that 'reconciled' writers all too often lack.[28]

'Home is so Sad' achieves in detail the exactness of poise Larkin describes above. And we cannot help noticing the diction of his reference to death as a 'screaming close-up'. In what is probably more than a coincidence, the speaker in 'The Old Fools' asks, 'Why aren't they screaming?' The qualified extent to which he can answer the question is intimately connected, as we have seen, with the simultaneous realisation of the suggestions of beauty in life that were presented in the old people's memories and in the abundant possibilities described as 'the million-petalled flower of being here'. Failure and death in his world are undeniably, and often bitterly, present and demand candid attention. Yet they are not there only as morbid realities, since they provoke, in representative poems such as 'Home is so Sad' and 'The Old Fools', a more sober registration of the value of life and a struggling hope that moments of beauty are valuable beyond their immediate sensation.

Larkin's predisposition toward beauty mitigates his sadness and keeps it from falling to mere spiritual fatigue. It is obvious that the early *The North Ship* is quite pale, not to mention unconsciously amusing, in its youthful and contrived sadness – 'There is regret. Always, there is regret' (*NS*, p. 37) – but the poet's more considered sadness after that volume is consistently in touch with the further seriousness he has analysed in Hardy and Betjeman's works, and it remains in his canon as an important sentiment. In *High Windows* this form of seriousness is particularly emphatic to the convictions in 'Sad Steps', 'The Trees' and 'Cut Grass', and, to settle on a single example, the last poem very concisely enacts his stated concerns with the emotion:

> Cut grass lies frail:
> Brief is the breath
> Mown stalks exhale.
> Long, long the death
>
> It dies in the white hours
> Of young-leafed June
> With chestnut flowers,
> With hedges snowlike strewn,
>
> White lilac bowed,
> Lost lanes of Queen Anne's lace,
> And the high-builded cloud
> Moving at a summer's pace.

(*HW*, p. 41)

Sadness and beauty comingle here in a subdued moment of careful observation in which a recognised fragility in the natural world is also captured as a human metaphor at the same time. The building-up of rich images moves from the close sensation of the 'cut grass' to the more cosmic reach of the 'high-builded cloud', an image which analogously echoes the soft beauty of the 'chestnut flowers' and the 'Lost lanes of Queen Anne's lace'. The rhyming of images, Hopkinsesque in its form, aids the evocation of a moment of sad praise which unites the human and the natural world by a controlling perception of transience. While the groundtone of the piece is a sad one, the sensitivity to beauty is inseparable from the speaker's very quietly stated perception of the universality of pain in the universe.

'Cut Grass' is a calm and a very lucid poem and its pessimism is given a maturity by its inductive method of justifying its emotion of sadness. Perhaps one of the more fragile of Larkin's recent statements on the universality of suffering, it nevertheless surpasses that kind of criticism which merely abjures the emotion of sadness because confident that sadness is the mark of a withdrawn and self-absorbed personality, an immature one. After *The North Ship*, Larkin's sadness – when present at all in the poems – carries with it the strengths of his awareness of the example of Hardy and Betjeman. It is a concious tone in his work and is the index of his respect and sympathy for a human condition governed by the rush of the hourglass and the inevitability of the scythe.

As a poet who explores experience while also engaging in self-doubt and self-criticism, Larkin continually invites the reader into the pleasure of second thoughts and emotional reappraisals of attitudes. There is a range to his voice and it includes modulations that are audible as tones of humour, wit, sadness, compassion, praise and celebration. The fact that he has remarked that 'depression is to me as daffodils were to Wordsworth'[29] should not be taken as his final word on his poetic personality, since a considerable dimension of his poetry moves beyond depression and toward other effects.

I have been using the term 'established personality' throughout my text thus far; and it is time to point to the source of that usage. Larkin is an impersonal poet in the dramatic sense that the tension between poet and persona in his poetry as a whole transcends the confines of established personality and moves the poetry into the order of a more inclusive objectivity. When D. W. Harding described the impersonality of Isaac Rosenberg's poetry he well captured this quality of further involvement in a diction that I have found eminently, if inadvertently, illuminating of Larkin's kind of personal statement. Of Rosenberg, Harding said,

> This willingness – and ability – to let himself be new-born into a new situation, not subduing his experience to his established personality, is a large part, if not the whole secret of the robustness which characterizes his best work. . . . It was Rosenberg's exposure of his whole personality that gave his work its quality of impersonality.[30]

While Larkin's established personality is arguably a depressed one – depression is the compost in many of his poems – he continually moves past that predisposition in the name of more complicated truths and a deeper self.

'Every poem', he has said more than once, 'starts out as either true or beautiful. Then you try to make the true ones seem beautiful, and the beautiful ones seem true.'[31] He proposes to value the beautiful in life without denying the 'true' and depressing aspects of experience, so it is unfortunate that his pessimism has not only been exaggerated into a singular focus by many of his critics, but also distracted us from the careful interplay in his volumes between bleakness and beauty.

Yet we should beware of erring in the opposite direction as well, since part of the achievement of Larkin's poetry lies in its candid portrayal of the 'true', of the failing aspects of the human condition, and of the grounds for an existential and social pessimism in our day. And I think it is more valuable, as a reading-experience, to search out the reasons for Larkin's pessimism than merely to disparage him because he is not a lotus-eater or a poet who is easily reconciled into a marketable joy. We see part of the rationale of Larkin's pessimism in his high regard for, and imitation of, Hardy's philosophy of sadness, but the further dimension of his unillusioned aspects as a poet take much of their wisdom, I think, from as analytical a poet of bleakness as Dr Samuel Johnson. It is when we read Larkin in the context of his neo-Augustan mannerisms as a poet that the full strength of his bleakness begins to emerge. Larkin's pessimism is not something to be disparaged or evaded; it is, rather, one of the benchmarks of his status as a major contemporary poet.

3 Hunger of the Imagination

Until recently it has been customary and sensible to discuss Larkin's bearing as a 'less deceived' poet in the midst of allusion to his filiations with Thomas Hardy and the Movement writers. It goes without saying, at this point, that Larkin's sensibility is congenial to the existential sadness of Hardy's vision and his more deflating effects as a sarcastic and ironic poet will always assure him a connection, however tenuous, with the Movement writers. But the more illuminating commentary on Larkin's 'less deceived' identity as a poet takes us behind the Movement poets' practice, to notice the new classical underpinnings of their anti-romanticism, their classical restraint. The dialectic of Larkin's poetry is inclusive of both romantic and ironic points of reference. And in the unillusioned dimension of his work as a whole it is the Augustan example held up by certain Movement writers which sifts down in his work as a residual habit of perception.

Many of the Movement writers, and Donald Davie most notably and analytically, admired the Augustan poets for their clear diction and employment of received or traditional poetic structures. Because of the anti-romantic and restrained implications of these strategies of craft, the Augustans were considered as mentors whose example might serve as antidote to the bohemianism of the poets of the 1940s, and the ostensibly uncontrolled romanticism of poets such as Dylan Thomas particularly.[1] In his *The Art of Philip Larkin* (1981), Simon Petch takes note of Larkin's broad affinities with Dr Johnson, and it remains, I think, to pursue that connection in more detail.[2] It is a connection which has the advantage of highlighting Larkin's analytical dimensions as a 'less deceived' poet and his effects as a poet of social satire.

Very like the Dr Johnson of 'The Vanity of Human Wishes' and *The History of Rasselas, Prince of Abissinia*, Larkin shows that there is a large territory of his sensibility which is Olympian in its unillusioned perspective in that it is attentive to the nature of the mind and the manifestations of mental illusions in society as a whole. Larkin, like Johnson, is critical of what Johnson calls in *Rasselas* a 'hunger of the imagination which preys incessantly upon life'. Many of his poems see us as victims of imaginative desire and as living primarily in a world of ambitions and dreams. In 'A Study of Reading Habits' Larkin satirises the literature of heroism and fulfilled promises, literature that is irrelevant to our lives. While he has no illusions about the comforts of the 'less deceived' mentality – its battle with cynicism and the jaded personality, its debilitating effects on one's impulse to celebration and wonder – many of his poems explore the pains of that habit of mind which is always reaching, as Johnson has put it, into 'boundless futurity'. Both Johnson and Larkin give weight and experiential texture to the idea that there is a boredom at the core of existence, and that it stimulates a daily spiritual condition in which the mind 'dances from scene to scene, unites all pleasures in all combinations, and riots in delights which nature and fortune, with all their bounty, cannot bestow'.[3] This habit of dreaming into the future, encouraged further by popular culture in the present day, is the central target of Larkin's more analytical pessimistic poems.

If we think also of Larkin's treatment of such themes as failure, the fragility of human choices (between bachelorhood and marriage, for instance), the importance of vocation in life, the horrifying reality of death, the struggles of common humanity, and the universality of human misery and sadness, it is obvious that he echoes many of Johnson's concerns as they have bearing on contemporary life. But it is primarily in his analysis of the workings of the human mind, the vanity of human wishes, that Larkin can be said to have found an analytical formula for this 'less deceived' poetry, and it is one which encourages him in the cleansing scepticism of his satirical works.

In terms of craft it is in his formal traditionalism as a writer that we see his rudimentary affinities with Johnson and the Augustan example. As a poet of traditional form he demonstrates in the very sinew of his craft the conservatism or classicism of his artistic temperament. As a poet who accepts the demands of stanzaic structures – while at the same time managing a colloquial ease in the speaking voice – he demonstrates that there is a limit to which the imagination must be held. Richard Murphy is in all likelihood correct in his conjecture that many still see Larkin as a poet who 'fluffs up the wings of dead ducks',[4] because of his adherence to traditional forms; and, as Simon Petch and John Reibetanz have both argued in detail, Larkin's playing-off of set forms against internal variations and original local effects arguably breathes new life into old forms which many assumed were defunct a long time ago.[5] For all of that, the point remains that Larkin's habitual use of traditional structures is the clearest signature in his craft that there is a strong conservative strain in his sensibility. In a model way, and in a manner which gives evidence of his affinity with Johnson's concern with the hunger of the imagination, that respect for restraint is perhaps most purely visible in 'Wires', a poem which exists close to the actual and also the moral centre of *The Less Deceived*:

> The widest prairies have electric fences,
> For though old cattle know they must not stray
> Young steers are always scenting purer water
> Not here but anywhere. Beyond the wires
>
> Leads them to blunder up against the wires
> Whose muscle-shredding violence gives no quarter.
> Young steers become old cattle from that day,
> Electric limits to their widest senses.

(*LD*, p. 27)

The conservative dimension of the poem lies thematically in its advocacy of a caution of mind. Its 'true' view of reality, that is, advocates a mature, a practical scepticism, and it could even be said to be quite instructive, given to a moral earnestness on the point. The figurative dimension of the work is there in the images of expanse and limitation that Larkin manages to freshen with the (potentially cliché) controlling metaphor of the fences, a metaphor which is enlivened with the adjectival particularities given in the second stanza. More than any other detail of form, none the less, the tight stanzaic pattern, its rhyme scheme and adherence to the iambic-pentameter metrical norm, serves to dramatise the intensity of the poet's respect for the conservative view: the poem both laments restriction and instructs us on the immaturity of attempting to live elsewhere than in the world of here and now.

The immaturity of living elsewhere than in the world of here and now is given more general and also more human bearing in *The Less Deceived* in the appositely titled 'Next, Please', a poem which can profitably be read as another example of Larkin's affinity with Johnson:

> Always too eager for the future, we
> Pick up bad habits of expectancy.
> Something is always approaching; every day
> *Till then* we say,
>
> Watching from a bluff the tiny, clear,
> Sparkling armada of promises draw near.
> How slow they are! And how much time they waste,
> Refusing to make haste!
>
> Yet still they leave us holding wretched stalks
> Of disappointment, for, though nothing balks
> Each big approach, leaning with brassware prinked,
> Each rope distinct,
>
> Flagged, with the figurehead with golden tits
> Arching our way, it never anchors; it's
> No sooner present than it turns to past.
> Right to the last
>
> We think each one will heave to and unload
> All good into our lives, all we are owed
> For waiting so devoutly and so long.
> But we are wrong:
>
> Only one ship is seeking us, a black-
> Sailed unfamiliar, towing at her back
> A huge and birdless silence. In her wake
> No waters breed or break.

(LD, p. 20)

Larkin's continuous appreciation of the Johnsonian anatomy of the mind is carried into poems in *The Whitsun Weddings* such as 'Days', where the speaker asks 'What are days for? / Days are where we live', and he laments the fact, satirically imaged, that neither religion nor medicine are helpful to us in answering 'Where can we live but days?' (*WW*, p. 27). 'Next, Please' participates in this kind of a discussion. As in Larkin's 'Triple Time', from *The Less Deceived*, it is a poem which is tonally almost incredulous in its recognition that for the human being 'the present' is 'A time traditionally soured, / A time unrecommended by event' (*LD*, p. 35).

Quite typically, Larkin brings his compassion to bear on the discovered anatomy of the mind that makes 'Next, Please' central to his affinity with Johnson. He understands the hunger of the human imagination as being both unfortunately natural ('habits of expectancy') and as an ultimate desire for perfection, for existential peace or transcendence of the spiritual scarcity of life. 'Next, Please' thoroughly demonstrates the classical restraint of his sceptical mentality also by token of its familiar adherence to the patterned stanza form. It is a pattern in which the rhyming of couplets is just audible enough to state the wit that leavens the sadness and the compassion in the tone.

In 'Next, Please' the poet's sympathy with the 'habits of expectancy', his recognition of the naturalness and frustration of the mentality, is signified also by the third-person-plural inclusion of himself in the malady. And it is also owned by the poet in the enacted yearning of emotion that he makes pictorially visible in the beauty of the ship of dreams. There is an obvious desire here, on Larkin's part, to involve himself in an error of thinking which he must finally see from a more mature height. Disciplined and careful as the stanzaic pattern is, it is none the less flexible enough to capture the emotional yearning, in the way the spilling sentences of the stanzas loosen those stanzas and unite them in a sensation of understanding involvement. As is usual with Larkin, he shows himself to be part of the human failure he examines. He does not shy away from his own humanity, with all of its related failures, in 'Next, Please', and the result is a poem which is profoundly emotional and analytical at the same stroke.

This willingness to participate in the universal longing of the human, if only in local effects, betokens the poet's understanding – one almost says forgiveness – of the imaginative hunger of us all, even if the bluntness of the couplets in the last stanza of 'Next,

Please' demonstrates the inevitability of Larkin's arrival at a cleansing scepticism, a 'less deceived' mentality when all is said and done. The pessimism of the poem is strong in both the beauty of the language and in the implicit positives which are distilled out of its understanding. As in 'Wires', a cliché (in this case the ship that is always coming in later) is stimulated into new life by the technical cleverness of the poem's internal effects of form. There is also a marginal extent to which 'Next, Please' turns D. H. Lawrence's 'ship of death' into a valuable allusive presence. In that faint echo from Lawrence we are positively reminded of the value of confronting mortality, the brevity of life, and the need to live it in accordance with such basic but neglected perceptions. For, Lawrence's 'The Ship of Death' appreciates the immediacy of living and it prizes the here and now, the present, in a way which is a positive corollary to Johnson's and Larkin's view of time and the human condition.

The value of the longer perspective – a view which foreshortens time and assesses life backwards from the perspective of the grave – is a strong habit of thinking in Johnson, Hardy and Lawrence, different as these writers otherwise are. Larkin has obviously absorbed the wisdom of that glance, and it is Johnson who most explicitly seems to have given him the analytical vigour with which to account for so much human frustration and spiritual failure.

Larkin is thoroughgoing, relentless, in the degree to which he includes himself in his perception of the natural wildness of human fancy. In 'Reasons for Attendance', 'Toads', 'Poetry of Departures', 'I Remember, I Remember', in *The Less Deceived*, and in 'Toads Revisited', 'A Study of Reading Habits' and 'Dockery and Son' in *The Whitsun Weddings*, he brings the power of illusion to bear on consideration of his own choices in life. In these poems he acknowledges that neither the settled life of accepted forms of success nor the more romantic life of the open road or the lonely artist include guarantees of happiness. In each of these poems, nevertheless, it is the witty poet of the more conservative temperament who overcomes or subdues the beckonings of the fancy.

'Poetry of Departures', a poem titled in a diction which places it in cluster with Larkin's other works on the call of elsewhere, mimics the tension visible in 'Next, Please' in that it generously re-creates, in an appealing imagery, the speaker's stock of dreams

and illusions before sweeping them out of the mind as so much
mental rubbish. So the first stanza is tonally exuberant in its
involvement in the zest of somebody else's rebellion against the
settled life. When someone tells us about someone who '*chucked up
everything* / And just cleared off', it is usual, says the speaker, that
the person is

> Certain you approve
> This audacious, purifying,
> Elemental move.
>
> And they are right, I think.
> We all hate home
> And having to be there:
> I detest my room,
> Its specially-chosen junk,
> The good books, the good bed,
> And my life, my perfect order:
> So to hear it said
>
> *He walked out on the whole crowd*
> Leaves me flushed and stirred,
> Like *Then she undid her dress*
> Or *Take that you bastard*;
> Surely I can, if he did?
> And that helps me stay
> Sober and industrious.
> But I'd go today,
>
> Yes, swagger the nut-strewn roads,
> Crouch in the fo'c'sle
> Stubbly with goodness, if
> It weren't so artificial,
> Such a deliberate step backwards
> To create an object:
> Books; china; a life
> Reprehensibly perfect.

                                        (*LD*, p. 34)

Life is limitation. While the speaker envies and begrudges the

freedom he hears about 'fifth hand', he knows that if it is pursued
with the low romantic expectation of perfection and fulfilment it
actually does little more than seek an order which is already
available in the conservative mythology of the settled life. The
scorn of false romanticism is only a small degree sharper than the
self-mockery evident in the speaker's disparagement of his own
neat and vulnerable choice; and, as in 'Toads', where there is a
similar scorn for 'the stuff / That dreams are made on' (*LD*,
p. 32), the consent to limitation – so evident in the tight
traditional form of the poem – is not without its enacted yearning
after the dreamed of possibilities of experience which are prized
before they are rejected with analysis. It is usual for Larkin in his
poetry of ironic realism to opt for the conservative choice, to insist
that 'Days are where we live' (*WW*, p. 27). Yet he almost
invariably opts for that choice amidst an expression of self-
mockery and only after he has created images of fanciful
happiness which (in their very attractiveness) demonstrate his
own hungers.

Larkin is not insensitive to the compelling nature of the world of
dream and illusion. He understands the basis of such dreams,
their natural growth out of boredom and the desire for perfection.
But he holds to the need for imaginative restraint because as an
ironic realist he recognises that there is a modicum of truth in the
grim claim of Johnson's Imlac that 'Human life is everywhere a
state in which much is to be endured, and little to be enjoyed',[6]
despite the fact that he has objected to Modernist art because 'it
helps us neither to enjoy nor endure'.[7] Poetry should at least
struggle for some kind of imaginative compensation.

And Larkin's art, even at its darkest, does so. He lightens his
satire with a low-key humour, and his surgical attempts to unbend
the mind from its worst and most self-deceptive habits of thought
are, like Johnson's before him, not only severe in the name of a
spiritual health but also stated as a toughly intelligent response to
human misery. Larkin might be humorous in his treatment of
illusions much of the time, but in instances such as 'Deceptions' he
shows that he sees the part they play in the victimisation of us all.
In response to the grief of the eighteenth-century rape victim in
that poem, he says 'Even so distant, I can taste your grief', and

> Slums, years, have buried you. I would not dare
> Console you if I could. What can be said,

Except that suffering is exact, but where
Desire takes charge, readings will grow erratic?
For you would hardly care
That you were less deceived, out on that bed,
Than he was, stumbling up the breathless stair
To burst into fulfilment's desolate attic.

(*LD*, p. 37)

In the uncollected poem 'Breadfruit', Larkin speaks of how 'absolute / Maturity falls' because of the tenacity of 'dream[s] / Of native girls' that persist on into old age. They persist because they are 'uncorrected visions' in spite of the contrary reality of more ordinary, prosaic life as seen without the haze of dream by the mature sceptic. Being unillusioned, as the lives of Larkin's sceptical speakers clearly demonstrate, is not a guarantee of happiness; but it is the view of Johnson in 'The Vanity of Human Wishes' and Larkin in a whole cluster of his poems that, while illusions are sometimes comforting, they also have a tendency to compound misery and increase the spiritual squalor of life. Illusions can sharpen disillusionment, as they do in 'Deceptions', where there is that resonating 'burst into fulfilment's desolate attic'. Illusions can as readily create human suffering and unbridled desires as they can create warm dreams. A source of surplus human unhappiness, they need to be diminished.

When Larkin's ironic persona is employed as a visor through which to view contemporary society, what is seen is something which heightens the poet's gift for scorn. He sees the public's innate human hunger of the imagination manipulated by the bad poetry of a commercial conspiracy which promises unalloyed happiness. His conservative nostalgia as a poet who attempts to preserve the beauty of the past and his clarity as a Johnsonian analyst of the human mind play significant roles in his poetry about the urban reality of the contemporary world.

His indictment of contemporary culture is passive in its nostalgia for a more rooted culture of the past, but it is energetic and detailed in its severe depiction of the reasons for cultural decline. In 'MCMXIV', the poet regrets the loss of innocence and artificial charm which the event of the Great War seems to have marked off for so many writers since that time. Thinking of the leisurely and poetic sense of unity in Edwardian culture he laments,

> Never such innocence,
> Never before or since,
> As changed itself to past
> Without a word – the men
> Leaving the gardens tidy,
> The thousands of marriages
> Lasting a little while longer:
> Never such innocence again.

> (*WW*, p. 28)

This relatively forlorn speaker is but one, somewhat Betjeman-esque, variation on the conservative Larkin who demonstrates a sharpened tone in his satirical social poems, ones such as the much later 'Going, Going', in *High Windows*. 'Going, Going' envisages a future which, on the evidence of the present, appears to be heading for little more than a grotesque parody of the society nostalgically portrayed in 'MCMXIV'. The present is decadent by comparison, an unbeautiful commercial travesty in which the desires of the many are exploited by the cynicism of a few:

> The crowd
> Is young in the M1 cafe;
> Their kids are screaming for more –
> More houses, more parking allowed,
> More caravan sites, more pay.
> On the Business Page, a score

> Of spectacled grins approve
> Some takeover bid that entails
> Five per cent profit (and ten
> Per cent more in the estuaries): move
> Your works to the unspoilt dales
> (Grey area grants)! And when

> You try to get near the sea
> In summer . . .

> It seems, just now,
> To be happening so very fast;
> Despite all the land let free
> For the first time I feel somehow
> That it isn't going to last,
>
> That before I snuff it, the whole
> Boiling will be bricked in
> Except for the tourist parts –
> First slum of Europe: a role
> It won't be hard to win,
> With a cast of crooks and tarts.

(*HW*, pp. 21–2)

The scenario goes past English regionality by virtue of its portrayal of a familiar materialism on the move – and, to borrow a famous Lawrentian question, where does the 'go' go to? In Larkin's poem it is headed for a physical future in which 'all that remains / For us will be concrete and tyres' (*HW*, p. 22). England in the present is seen as governed spiritually by a sort of public rocking-horse winner which is 'screaming for more'; but it is the 'cast of crooks and tarts' who are condemned more than the victims of the commercially implanted values. Much of the caustic satire in 'Going, Going' is expressed in the name of memory, memory of the now only remnant culture of the past, the 'meadows, the lanes, / The guildhalls, the carved choirs' which are overcome by 'greeds and garbage' that makes up the approaching future. He softens his attack – and also his certainty about the analysis – by adding the conclusion that

> Most things are never meant.
> This won't be, most likely: but greeds
> And garbage are too thick-strewn
> To be swept up now, or invent
> Excuses that make them all needs.
> I just think it will happen, soon.

(*HW*, p. 22)

In the analytical framework of Larkin's poetry of the popular imagination, it is a reigning commercial mythology, one very shrewd in its ability to 'invent / Excuses that make them all needs', which comes in for his harshest satirical scorn.

Larkin's abstractions about the debilitation of contemporary culture by commercial values are embedded in his poems at the level of the experiential, the immediate sensations of daily life. They grow from, rather than are imposed upon the felt life of his individual poems. But they are guided, too, by Johnson's analysis of the mind as given to hungers of fancy and they cumulatively exist as an indictment of the bad poetry of a materialistic society. In *The Modern Century* (1967) Northrop Frye speaks of the imaginative scarcity of the modern world, and in his definition of what he terms 'stupid realism' he inadvertently frames the cultural mentality which Larkin's Johnsonian understanding of the mind is intent upon exposing as a source of imaginative decadence, and also as a stimulus to common grief and disappointment. Frye remarks,

> By stupid realism I mean what is actually a kind of sentimental idealism, an attempt to present a conventionally attractive or impressive appearance as an actual or attainable reality. Thus it is a kind of parody or direct counter-presentation to prophetic realism. We see it in the vacuous pretty-girl faces of advertising, in the clean-limbed athletes of propaganda magazines, in the haughty narcissism of shop-window mannequins, in the heroically transcended woes of soap-opera heroines, in eulogistic accounts of the lives of celebrities, usually those in entertainment, in the creation by Madison Avenue of a wise and kindly father-figure out of some political stooge, and so on.[8]

In such anti-commercial poems as 'Breadfruit', 'Sunny Prestatyn' and 'Essential Beauty', Larkin angrily attacks the false Platonism or stupid realism which Frye gathers together in the imagery of his comments above. In the process of attacking such fraudulence, he gives breathing presence to life lived according to the dominant imaginative hungers of the familiar contemporary world.

The frustrations created by stupid realism are understood in 'Sunny Prestatyn' in the violence that is soon done to a poster which looks and reads like the following:

> *Come To Sunny Prestatyn*
> Laughed the girl on the poster,
> Kneeling up on the sand
> In tautened white satin.
> Behind her, a hunk of coast, a
> Hotel with palms
> Seemed to expand from her thighs and
> Spread breast-lifting arms.

> (*WW*, p. 35)

Like the poster images of 'native girls who bring breadfruit, / Whatever they are' in 'Breadfruit', the 'girl on the poster' is significantly portrayed as a pure form from elsewhere, one of the 'vacuous pretty-girl faces of advertising' designed to set in motion the hunger of the imagination which can be turned into ready profit. The descending stanzas of the poem describe the violence done to the poster by graffiti, a violence which is relished by Larkin primarily, it would appear, because it states a healthy rebellion against the fact that 'She was too good for this life'. Finally, within two weeks of the poster having been put up,

> Someone had used a knife
> Or something to stab right through
> The moustached lips of her smile.
> She was too good for this life.
> Very soon, a great transverse tear
> Left only a hand and some blue.
> Now *Fight Cancer* is there.

> (*WW*, p. 35)

It is, of course, the 'less deceived' mentality of the rebellious graffiti which captures Larkin's praise: there is a phantom sceptic out there somewhere who is sarcastic, unillusioned and satirical. Larkin adds to his celebration of the act a resonating irony in the observation that 'Now *Fight Cancer* is there', as it was precisely the cancer of bad poetry, of stupid realism, which the graffiti were battling with an ironic vengeance.

Nevertheless, if the graffiti oddly signify a critical capacity in the common man, Larkin more often sees ordinary humanity as the victim of the commercial dreams. The youths in 'Breadfruit', for example, dream on into old age, and learn nothing whatsoever from the discrepancy between their erotic dreams and the details of their lives. They continue to 'dream / Of native girls who bring breadfruit', and

> Such uncorrected visions end in church
> > Or registrar:
> A mortgaged semi- with a silver birch;
> Nippers: the widowed mum; having to scheme
> With money; illness; age. So absolute
> Maturity falls, when old men sit and dream
> Of naked native girls who bring breadfruit,
> > Whatever they are.

The power of the fantasy, as the sarcastic last line makes explicit, lies in the fact that the dreams are purely removed from the confines of 'A mortgaged semi- with a silver birch' and all that this magnificently concise image signifies. Perhaps there is a bit of the bachelor's contempt for marriage involved here (others of Larkin's poems are satirical of bachelorhood), but a tendency in the speaker toward caricatures does not diminish a sense of pathos which Larkin manages here along with his sarcasm.

That sense of pathos, suffering with the victim, is more solid, I think, in poems such as 'Afternoons', where he also juxtaposes romantic dreams, chiefly inspired by popular culture, with the more prosaic reality of domestic fact. The women in this poem are aging housewives, and as they stand waiting for their children, who are set 'free' to play at swing and sandpit in a recreation ground, the speaker remarks,

> Behind them, at intervals,
> Stand husbands in skilled trades,
> An estateful of washing,
> And the albums, lettered
> *Our Wedding*, lying
> Near the television:
> Before them, the wind
> Is ruining their courting-places.

> (*WW*, p. 44)

What they individually represent is the ordinary humanity who, like the Mr Bleaneys of the world, have 'no more to show / Than one hired box' (*WW*, p. 10). There is a desperate quality of boredom in their lives and it is partly grounded in their relative poverty and the fact that they are the victims of the commercial mythology of their day. They are similar to the working-class people, as in the 'cobble-close families / In mill-towns on dark mornings', for whom 'life is slow dying' (*WW*, p. 11), and the lower middle class who are viewed in 'Here' as 'the cut-price crowd', the 'residents from raw estates' who are

> brought down
> The dead straight miles by stealing flat-faced trolleys,
> Push through plate-glass swing doors to their desires –
> Cheap suits, red kitchen-ware, sharp shoes, iced lollies,
> Electric mixers, toasters, washers, driers. . . .

> (*WW*, p. 9).

And their 'desires' are manipulated by the stupied realism, victimised by the commercial art of the popular imagination.

It is on behalf of this ordinary humanity that Larkin's satire of the bad poetry of our day exists. While on occasion it might appear that his anger is expressed merely out of his nostalgia for a more beautiful past, the more expansive reality, one that includes most of his poems about contemporary life, is that his anger includes a compassion for the ordinary humanity which is victimised by the dream pictures of life, enslaved by the sentimental idealism which permeates the streetscapes and the mindscape of the contemporary world. That compassion is best assured as a sentiment in 'Essential Beauty', where the idealised images on the billboards are contrasted with the actuality of life below, and a poetry of the real is valued over the lies of third-rate art:

> In frames as large as rooms that face all ways
> And block the ends of streets with giant loaves,
> Screen graves with custard, cover slums with praise
> Of motor-oil and cuts of salmon, shine
> Perpetually these sharply-pictured groves
> Of how life should be. High above the gutter

A silver knife sinks into golden butter,
A glass of milk stands in a meadow, and
Well-balanced familes, in fine
Midsummer weather, owe their smiles, their cars
Even their youth, to that small cube each hand
Stretches towards. These, and the deep armchairs
Aligned to cups at bedtime, radiant bars
(Gas or electric), quarter-profile cats
By slippers on war mats,
Reflect none of the rained-on streets and squares

They dominate outdoors. Rather, they rise
Serenely to proclaim pure crust, pure foam,
Pure coldness to our live imperfect eyes
That stare beyond this world, where nothing's made
As new or washed quite clean, seeking the home
All such inhabit. There, dark raftered pubs
Are filled with white-clothed ones from tennis-clubs,
And the boy puking his heart out in the Gents
Just missed them, as the pensioner paid
A halfpenny more for Granny Graveclothes' Tea
To taste old age, and dying smokers sense
Walking towards them through some dappled park
As if on water that unfocused she
No match lit up, nor drag ever brought near,
Who now stands newly clear,
Smiling, and recognising, and going dark.

(*WW*, p. 42)

The billboards not only block out reality, 'Screen graves with custard, cover slums with praise'; they remake the actual world into a surreal landscape composed of oversized lumpish Platonic objects such as glasses of milk in meadows and cosy domestic settings on top of the 'rained-on streets and squares', reflecting (using the poem's own wording) nothing of the literal but a great deal of the moral–imaginative life of the actual world. The 'well-balanced families', that idealisation Marshall McLuhan mocks in *The Mechanical Bride* (1951), have nothing whatever to do with the reality of the 'cobble-close families / In mill-towns on dark mornings' (*WW*, p. 11); like all of the other images on the billboards they are 'pure crust, pure foam', sentimental portraits of an almost religious beyond, a place where an absolute home exists in transcendence of the bleaker reality of the literal environment. The lengthy sentence structures in the first stanza, their wandering as they build the images (Larkin makes it look as though he has only to list them), rhythmically enact the motion of the seduction upward, before the poem turns toward the irony which begins descent.

The ironic contrasts in the last stanza are devastating in the effectiveness of their oppositions between the world of fantasy and the world of fact. The liquor-drinking 'white-clothed ones from tennis clubs', who seem to walk straight out of F. Scott Fitzgerald's world, are in ironic contrast with the nauseated youth in the pub lavatory. And the goddess of cigarettes from the 'dappled park', from what is earlier called one of 'these sharply-pictured groves', is 'newly clear' to the 'dying smokers', the victims of the seductive imagery, the 'stupid realism' of the billboards.

The poise of Larkin's satire, as opposed to its logical machinery, exists in the combined irony and compassion with which his analysis proceeds. His satire exists in the name of the ordinary, reduced humanity of the sub-heroic characters in the last stanza. And, although the title 'Essential Beauty' is loaded with irony and a mockery of the false Platonism of the billboards, it serves up a different meaning in relation to humanity itself. The poem recognises that what adds insult to injury in all of this is that the very success of the commercial manipulation of the images lies partly in their ability to twist a genuine human hunger for 'essential beauty' away from the religious or philosophical and toward the secular aim of sheer profit; so the manipulation is dehumanising in the extreme. It preys on genuine hungers and perverts them to its own cynical motivations.

There are images of getting and spending throughout Larkin's poetry of social satire, and those who 'Push through plate-glass swing doors to their desires' (*WW*, p. 9) are entering that most common substitute church in our day, the department store. In 'The Large Cool Store', Larkin describes the substitute church in a manner which resounds the insight into false Platonism in 'Essential Beauty' and simultaneously evokes in detail the unreal, almost religiose, atmosphere of this clean well-lighted place. 'The large cool store selling cheap clothes / Set out in simple sizes plainly' caters to the ordinary humanity who 'leave at dawn low terraced house / Timed for factory, yard and site', and what it sells to them in its 'Modes for Night' section is the dream of all fulfilment at once:

> Lemon, sapphire, moss-green, rose
> Bri-Nylon Baby-Dolls and Shorties
> Flounce in clusters. To suppose
> They share that world, to think their sort is
> Matched by something in it, shows
>
> How separate and unearthly love is,
> Or women are, or what they do,
> Or in our young unreal wishes
> Seem to be: synthetic, new,
> And natureless in ecstasies.

(WW, p. 30)

It is the vanity of these and other 'young unreal wishes' which are a common source of disillusionment in Larkin's poems about the social imagination. The commercialised landscape of his world is one in which an artificial heaven is promised by the 'stupid realism' of bad poetry, a poetry which dominates culture with images that are 'synthetic, new, / And natureless in ecstasies'. The most potent dream pictures in this culture are not artistic or religious in any rigorous sense of the word; they are the smooth images of commercial packaging, the 'pure crust, pure foam' (*WW*, p. 42) of a commercial mythology. It is not insignificant that the evangelist in 'Faith Healing' is described as 'Upright in rimless glasses, silver hair, / Dark suit, white collar' (*WW*, p. 15). In his dress, manners, speech and his profit-making, he is a Madison Avenue, packaged priest whose cynicism is as deep as his manipulation of imaginative hungers is effective. He is selling the same 'synthetic, new' supreme fictions which the large cool store houses in its function as a home for what, in the end, are eternal hungers of the imagination.

Larkin shares in those hungers even if quite obviously his own quest for beauty transcends the ironic beauty of the popular imagination by including it, and by taking the surgeon's knife to the pursuit of unalloyed happiness in the process. He is assuredly a poet of restraint, an analytical and neo-Augustan poet; and his creative scepticism as a writer can be measured partly by way of confrontation with his attempt, as an analyst of the imagination, to clear the mind of a great many illusions. In the end, there is an accountable integrity to his unillusioned pessimism and, like most rigorous sceptical writers, he substantiates the 'truth' value of his candid glance with the evidence of the living facts that surround him.

The danger the critic enters into by paying attention to the strenuousness of the poet's pessimism in these respects is a temptation to overstate the extent of the poet's unillusioned vision, its compelling signature as representative of Larkin's wider view. But Larkin's poetic personality is more capacious than an emphasis on his 'less deceived' poems alone will tend to convey. His energies as an ironic poet are most prominent in *The Less Deceived* and they persist in his later volumes as well, so it is partly understandable that this aspect of his personality and vision should have become the major identity his critics isolate as typical of his work. Yet, even within the darkness of his gloomier poems, there is always that compassion for humanity, the wit and humour, and, I have argued, an analytical vigour, which signify an energy and creativity in his pessimism which cannot be readily dismissed. Larkin, that is to say, does not require special pleading for his ironic energies as a poet, since an understanding of the contours of those energies demonstrates that his unillusioned works participate in an esteemed tradition.

And beauty remains in the poems already discussed, even if it is there as a nostalgic presence, or is seen as something broken or diminished by the reality the poet's honesty leads him to include. Beauty is also there in the shape and symmetry of the poetry itself, in spite of the pessimism of its contents. But, in any event, it is not in the poet's poetry of ironic realism that we should be looking for the finest expression of his energies as a poet of beauty. It is in his clusters of poetry about found beauty and the surprise of nature that we begin to witness his clearest focus on the 'other' reality, which also keeps his pessimism from being merely self-absorbed.

As we concentrate attention on Larkin's 'romantic' impulse as a poet, it is crucial that we take notice of the highly special use that the term must have in this context. In *The Movement* (1980), Blake Morrison reminds us that the Movement started as an anti-romantic phenomenom and it did so 'despite the fact that (especially in the cases of Larkin and Gunn) this to some extent meant going against instinctive inclinations'. He traces that only ostensible contradiction in the work of Donald Davie, and gives us the following thoughtful commentary from Davie's *The Poet in the Imaginary Museum*:

> we must be glad to be compelled to recognize that we are all, like it or not, post-Romantic people; that the historical developments which we label 'Romanticism' were not a series of aberrations which we can and should disown, but rather a sort of landslide which permanently transformed the mental landscape which in the twentieth century we inhabit, however reluctantly. It seems to me now that this was a recognition which I came to absurdly late in life; that my teachers when I was young encouraged me to think that I could expunge Romanticism from my historical past by a mere act of will or a stroke of the pen, and that by doing this I could climb back into the lost garden of the seventeenth century. It is not a question of what we want or like; it is what we are stuck with – post-Romantic is what we are.[9]

I think Larkin would agree with much of this, as he might also agree with D. J. Enright's reservations, asserted in 1955, about the imaginative and emotional limitations of Modernism:

> These poets [the Modernists], too, did not know enough – and their ignorance has proved remarkably infectious. They may have known what the Romantics were ignorant of, but they were ignorant of what the Romantics knew. In this aspect, as in others, Modernism seems to be a violent inversion of Romanticism: each is notably weak where the other is notably strong.[10]

Irony, like intelligence itself, isn't everything – just as wonder and emotion are limited by their tendency to simplification. Neither Davie nor Enright nor Larkin is being at all blunt about these matters; what the persistence of their respect for aspects of Romantic art shows, rather, is an ability to move their way past easy labels and recognise the difficult admixture in the contemporary poet's inheritance of traditions.

T. E. Hulme, a theorist of poetry whose work caught the

attention of certain Movement poets, becomes a helpful commentator in this context. In Hulme's definition of what he meant by the 'classical in verse', he speaks of the careful blend of irony and wonder which is the hallmark of the classical in verse, as he views it. One of the valuable aspects of that definition is its capacity for describing the poise of wonder which is the measure of a poet who is both ironic and romantic at the same time. In his definition of what he meant by the 'classic of motion', he makes a statement which comes close to being a perfect delineation of, and account for, Larkin's quality of imaginative restraint. It speaks of an intelligent control over romantic energies which is conservative without being inhibited:

> What I mean by classical in verse, then is this. That even in the most imaginative flights there is always a holding back, a reservation. The classical poet never forgets his finiteness, his limit as man. *He remembers always that he is mixed up with earth. He may jump, but he always returns back, he never flies away into the circumambient gas.*
>
> You might say if you wished that the whole of the romantic attitude seems to crystallise in verse round metaphors of flight. Hugo is always flying, flying over abysses, flying up into the eternal gases. The word infinite in every line.
>
> *In the classical attitude you never seem to swing right along to the infinite nothing.* If you say an extravagant thing which does exceed the limits inside which you know man to be fastened, yet there is always conveyed in some way at the end an impression of yourself standing outside it, and not quite believing it, or consciously putting it forward as a flourish. *You never go blindly into an atmosphere more than the truth*, an atmosphere too rarefied for man to breathe for long. You are always faithful to the conception of a limit.[11]

Hulme's words not only read as a gloss on Larkin's restraint as an ironic realist – a sceptical poet whose poetry is alert to the need for 'the conception of a limit' in craft and mind – but also, more importantly, describe an ambiguity which is dramatised in the moments of wonder which are central to the more romantic poems in his mature volumes. One can be unillusioned without being arid.

Larkin's tendency is to record his moment of mystical flight and at the same time hold back from the 'swing along to the infinite nothing'. And to demonstrate from poems we are already familiar with in other connections, there is, for example, the posture of the speaker at the end of 'Church Going', a man who remembers that he is 'mixed up with earth' even though he is also gesturing toward an eternal land of the spirit. His classical attitude holds him back from the conclusiveness of faith. After his praise of the residual sacredness of the place as a 'serious house on serious earth', he concludes,

> And that much can never be obsolete,
> Since someone will forever be surprising
> A hunger in himself to be more serious,
> And gravitating with it to this ground,
> Which, he once heard, was proper to grow wise in,
> If only that so many dead lie round.

> (*LD*, p. 29)

We are moved successfully into a rarefied 'atmosphere' in 'Church Going', but are returned to the 'conception of a limit'. The ironic turning-back leaves us soberly facing the graveyard, a perspective which underlines the need to be 'serious' just as it also prevents us from 'flying away into circumambient gas'. The restraint is there in the prison of the stanzaic pattern, and also in the realism of the speaker's empirical glance. It is romantic, in other words, but romantic in the manner of the cautious realism of which Hulme is speaking. There is an active polarity here which is creative.

In the concluding moment of 'High Windows', there is the same reining-in of the flight, the same recognition of the power of the 'atmosphere', and the same corresponding realisation that it is 'too rarefied for man to breathe for long':

> Rather than words comes the thought of high windows:
> The sun-comprehending glass,
> And beyond it, the deep blue air, that shows
> Nothing, and is nowhere, and is endless.

> (*HW*, p. 17)

The voice is both given to a flight into wonder, and ambiguously gesturing by including an image of the void. The precarious poise of the moment, its designed ambiguity, is as careful as anything which is conceivable in art; an experience of the boundless mystery of the universe is given as a moment of beauty, but with inclusion of a seriously ironic reserve in the allowance of a diminishing feeling of potential emptiness.

The wonder in 'High Windows' is therefore not as confident and mythically based as Shelley's otherwise very similar sense of wonder in these famous analogous lines:

> The One remains, the many change and pass;
> Heaven's light forever shines, Earth's shadows fly;
> Life, like a dome of many-coloured glass,
> Stains the white radiance of Eternity.[12]

Larkin's kind of wonder is more contemporary, is not underpinned by a Platonic mythic conviction. Hulme had said that 'Wonder can only be an attitude of a man passing from one stage to another, it can never be a permanently fixed thing.' Wonder was once encouraged by myths which became stale, and that is why 'A romantic movement must have an end of the very nature of the thing.'[13] What we have in its place is not simply irony (in any negative or inhibited sense) but the possibility of a creative–imaginative poetry of restraint, a poetry of passing wonder.

If Davie and Enright and a series of other post-war poets recognise the limits of Romanticism and are not entirely satisfied with the inhibition of the Modernists, what is available in Hulme's aesthetic is a scrupulous blending of irony and wonder into a realism which, I think, is central to Larkin's work as a whole. In the suggestive statement regarding his concern with a poetry of 'truth' and a poetry of 'beauty', a concern which is in tension in his own aesthetic, Larkin analogously states his own struggle with Hulme's dialectic:

> I have always believed that beauty is beauty, truth truth, that is not all ye know on earth nor all ye need to know, and I think a person usually starts off either from the feeling How beautiful that is or from the feeling How true that is. One of the jobs of the poem is to make the beautiful seem true and the true beautiful. . . .[14]

A belief in Keats's powerful aphorism is no longer possible, as Hulme so very well knew; but the two impulses remain since the hunger of the imagination, even in its lowest forms, continues to seek the wholeness of meaning which the aphorism so highly values.[15]

Hulme had the detailed perceptivity to see that, without a convincing mythology, it is not possible wholeheartedly to write a poetry of absolute truth and beauty at once. And, while many twentieth-century poets have attempted to revitalise the myths, others have settled instead for a poetry of passing wonder. In this context the example of D. H. Lawrence becomes important to Larkin, I think, because, like Lawrence, Larkin is a poet of immediacy, and a poet who portrays beauty in his works as a transient wonder at the mystery of the living world. For all of his scepticism and strenuous pessimism as a writer, he is wide awake to a remaining beauty in the surrounding world. And, if Hulme's aesthetic presents us with a critical diction with which to define the limits of that wonder, Lawrence is the artist whose example Larkin absorbs in the finer details of his lines. In short, I would argue, the 'other' Larkin is a Lawrentian one.

4 Solitary Wonder

In 1970 Larkin referred to a conversation he once had with Vernon Watkins in which 'we talked a good deal about poetry, or rather Vernon talked, in the main, and I listened: it was difficult to avoid the subject in his company. He did listen patiently to my enthusiasm for D. H. Lawrence. . . .'[1] The early enthusiasm was perhaps the eagerness of the younger Larkin, who was to demonstrate in *The North Ship* that he was a cloudily romantic poet. Nevertheless, the romantic impulse in Larkin's poetry survives the new scepticism of his volumes after *The North Ship*, and D. H. Lawrence's influence has much to do with its logic and its imagery. Larkin did not simply learn a new cynicism from Hardy and Johnson, a complacent pessimism. It is more accurate to say that their pessimistic visions of life sobered Larkin's romantic energies and led him to that honesty of perception which permeates his poetry of truth and poetry of beauty alike. Lawrence, on the other hand, has helped Larkin to sustain his sensitivity to beauty and to give shape to that talent in a significant way.

Lawrence has an effect on Larkin's concerns as a poet of the commonplace, and it is an effect which gives a positive temper to Larkin's social poetry of ritual community events. There is not only a 'less deceived' social poet in Larkin's volumes, but also a poet of social celebration who shares with Lawrence a gift for the rendition of human festivity. But these considerations are the topic of the next chapter. My main concern in these pages is with what I think is Larkin's first and most rudimentary connection with Lawrence: his strategy of evoking the living presence of the world and shaping such evocations into moments of passing wonder.

Only two of Larkin's poems are undeniably Lawrence-inspired. 'Wedding Wind' and 'The Explosion' are his only certain Lawrentian poems and it is telling that the former was first published in 1946, and the latter is the piece which ends *High*

Windows. They are both irregular to Larkin, at first glance. 'Wedding Wind' is an animated poem and it seems to stand out in *The Less Deceived*, where it competes with the surrounding scepticism of other poems. Nevertheless, it *is* a characteristic Larkin poem in that it shares with other Larkin poems of restraint an implicit reserve, a measure of realism which prevents its speaker from that soaring 'right along to the infinite nothing' of which Hulme speaks. The wonder in its detail is fleeting and 'mixed up with earth':

> The wind blew all my wedding-day,
> And my wedding-night was the night of the high wind;
> And a stable door was banging, again and again,
> That he must go and shut it, leaving me
> Stupid in candlelight, hearing rain,
> Seeing my face in the twisted candlestick,
> Yet seeing nothing. When he came back
> He said the horses were restless, and I was sad
> That any man or beast that night should lack
> The happiness I had.
>
>   Now in the day
> All's ravelled under the sun by the wind's blowing.
> He has gone to look at the floods, and I
> Carry a chipped pail to the chicken-run,
> Set it down, and stare. All is the wind
> Hunting through clouds and forests, thrashing
> My apron and the hanging cloths on the line.
> Can it be borne, this bodying-forth by wind
> Of joy my actions turn on, like a thread
> Carrying beads? Shall I be let to sleep
> Now this perpetual morning shares my bed?
> Can even death dry up
> These new delighted lakes, conclude
> Our kneeling as cattle by all-generous waters?

$$(LD, \text{p. } 15)$$

As a natural symbol of inner change, the wind is radical in its force and beauty. The bride's ecstasy is as profound as it is also unsettling, and Larkin is dealing with an experience here which is close to the religious. 'Religious feeling', he once remarked, 'should be more free of the accidents of time and place if it is to sound natural; it should not seem to require Tortoise stoves and box pews, nor be distracted by the wiring of a public address system.'[2] The intuitively religious implications of the bride's experience are immense yet are so without being drawn into abstract closure or conventional mythology. Her initial state is one of incredulity, and her happiness is bound to the earth by the feeling of reservation that also reflects the tentativeness of the creating mind behind the poem. The nervous insistence of the door 'banging, again and again' is the first of many reminders that she lives in a pressing reality of domestic necessity; her epiphany of joy is limited by its disjunction from the temporal reality of the surrounding environment. The first stanza precisely embodies the poet's claim that he wishes to write poems which are both true and beautiful, compelling yet realistic.

In the second stanza the wonder is made yet more nervous by the dissonance of the bride's sparse and violated surroundings. She questions whether it is possible to accommodate the depth of her happiness to the prosaic world of the 'chipped pail' and the 'hanging cloths' on the line. The grace of her experience, the sense of it as a religious experience, is temporary, passing. Like the wind it might leave her devastated, leave her like her surroundings 'ravelled under the sun', for, as with the brides in 'The Whitsun Weddings', she is involved in a ritual, a 'religious wounding' (*WW*, p. 22). The other fear, as the simile of the thread carrying beads suggests, is that the wonder is so extraordinary, and transcends so many of the details of her ordinary life; it makes life prematurely fulfilled and in an odd way unbearable. The religious possibilities of the experience, always present in the analogical structure of the lines ('candlelight', 'beads', 'kneeling as cattle', and so on), are emotionally gestured toward without being fully embraced.

The speaker reflects the poet's hesitation, his unwillingness conclusively to push the experience into eschatological truth. There is in the poem both a romantic and a restraining energy at once, a desire to move through the details of the living mystery with a tremendous power of imaginative suggestiveness, and at the same stroke to contain the experience, save it from resolution into certainty. 'Wedding Wind' is both interested in, and holds back from, the absolute. It shares with 'An Arundel Tomb' the 'almost-instinct almost true' hope that 'What will survive of us is love' (*WW*, p. 46). The 'happiness I had' of which the bride speaks is not cast ironically as a foolish pursuit of the unalloyed happiness central to the more sceptical poems in *The Less Deceived* but is rather dramatised as a powerful experience of wonder which is transient yet profound. Very similarly to Lawrence, Larkin refuses to 'nail down' the experience into a system of myth, but there is a residual hope for meaning in the poem that is disciplined by the admixture of 'truth' and 'beauty' and gives definition to the precarious wonder.

There is an unmistakably religious dimension to Larkin's legacy from Lawrence. For all of the fatigue of Christianity in the modern world, there is an imaginative and moral beauty in its mythology which Lawrence, like Larkin, finds compelling. Larkin names religion in 'Aubade' a 'vast moth-eaten musical brocade / Created to pretend we never die',[3] but this does not cancel our memory of the figure in 'Church Going', who demonstrates a longing for its ritual integrity, its past vitality. Further, in 'The Explosion', the last poem in *High Windows*, Larkin's durable respect for Christianity of the past is dramatised as a fulsome appreciation of its account for death and its fostering of a valuable sense of existential mystery. 'The Explosion' exists as a token of the longevity of Larkin's interest in Lawrence's imaginative example, and a solid example of Larkin's persistent concern with religious states of consciousness. As is the case with 'Wedding Wind', it is similarly dramatic in its registration of a state of being that is separate from the self, observed in the lives of others. The opening stanza of 'The Explosion' is thick with a sense of the ominous as 'Shadows pointed toward the pithead' and 'In the sun the slagheap slept'. Then,

> Down the lane came men in pitboots
> Coughing oath-edged talk and pipe-smoke,
> Shouldering off the freshened silence.
>
> One chased after rabbits; lost them;
> Came back with a nest of lark's eggs;
> Showed them; lodged them in grasses.
>
> So they passed in beards and moleskins,
> Fathers, brothers, nicknames, laughter,
> Through the tall gates standing open.

At noon there came a tremor; cows
Stopped chewing for a second; sun,
Scarfed as in heat-haze, dimmed.

The dead go on before us, they
Are sitting in God's house in comfort,
We shall see them face to face –

Plain as lettering in the chapels
It was said, and for a second
Wives saw men of the explosion

Larger than in life they managed –
Gold as on a coin, or walking
Somehow from the sun towards them,

One showing eggs unbroken.

(*HW*, p. 42)

The moment of awesome beauty rises inevitably from the coarse
details of the lives observed at the outset. The setting, atmosphere,
carefully controlled suspense, action and the concrete portrayal
of the men and their small gestures all accumulate into a
dramatisation which moves toward awe. The experience of the felt
life in the poem is, like that in 'Wedding Wind', domestic and
religious at the same time. The ambience of the piece is
Lawrentian right down to the detail of its variation on Lawrence's
hope for humanity as aristocrats of the sun which is given in the
image of the men 'Walking / Somehow from the sun towards
them'. The poem seeks and finds a purity of meaning and image
which grows out of the innocent lives it portrays. The religious
consciousness, centred in the minds of the wives in the descending
stanzas, gives birth to an atoned image of harmony and
perfection. Larkin is careful to qualify his own relationship to the
atoned view by placing the vision outside himself. He is careful,
that is, to resist a conclusive truth named 'Christian' and resists
turning the belief toward the reader for consent. 'The Explosion'
is as much about the value and psychology of faith as it is also
about the imaginatively compelling power of transcendent
meaning. 'Wedding Wind' and 'The Explosion' are the two

poems in Larkin's world which most clearly embody his ability to create centres of consciousness separate from himself. They are both poems of beauty and wonder and the inescapable affinity they share with Lawrence should suggest that their difference from so many of the poet's 'less deceived' writings demonstrate that the 'other' Larkin is a Lawrentian one.

Larkin's filiations with Lawrence are not limited to 'Wedding Wind' and 'The Explosion'. These two poems are simply the obvious cases in point. In their novelistic ability to move outside the self, their knowledge of human gesture as natural symbol, and their capacity for evoking wonder as an immediacy, they indicate Larkin's more obvious employment of Lawrence as a mentor. One is a very early poem and the other is the last poem in *High Windows*; and the less obvious, but certainly chartable, influence of Lawrence is pervasive in the many poems which exist in Larkin's chronicle between these two poems. For Larkin shares with Lawrence other, less obvious affinities and they have to do with his thematic concerns and with the imagery in his more solitary poetry involving nature.

We begin to notice the quieter affinities when we see that Larkin is inspired by Lawrence's ability to dramatise the universe as a living and beckoning presence. In all of Larkin's volumes – and more notably in the recent ones – there is a strong and revitalising sense of the natural world as conducive to a sense of mystery and as partly an answer to the poet's tendency toward pessimism and gloom. This is learned from Lawrence, I believe, and juxtaposition of a few lines from each poet would seem quickly to indicate a similarity of disposition and of imagery:

Space, of course, is alive
that's why it moves about;
and that's what makes it eternally spacious and unstuffy.

And somewhere it has a wild heart
that sends pulses even through me;
and I call it the sun;
and I feel aristocratic, noble, when I feel a pulse go through me
from the wild heart of space, that I call the sun of suns.

(Lawrence, 'Space'[4])

> Here is unfenced existence:
> Facing the sun, untalkative, out of reach.

> (Larkin, 'Here', *WW*, p. 9)

> And they attend me, dear translucent bergs:
> Silence and space.

> (Larkin, 'Age', *LD*, p. 30)

> And all the manifold blue, amazing eyes,
> The rainbow arching over in the skies,
> New sparks of wonder opening in surprise. . . .

> (Lawrence, 'Blueness'[5])

> Rather than words comes the thought of high windows:
> The sun-comprehending glass,
> And beyond it, the deep blue air, that shows
> Nothing, and is nowhere, and is endless.

> (Larkin, 'High Windows', *HW*, p. 17)

There are many passages in Larkin's and Lawrence's poetry which demonstrate their shared concern for the living presence of the elements, that 'Silence and space' which Larkin invokes in 'Age'. In their contemplative scope, many of Lawrence's poems reach wondrously outward to the integrity of the stars.[6] Similarly, an overlooked figure who is a variation on Larkin's romantic persona is the figure who stands contemplatively quiet at the end of 'Here' in *The Whitsun Weddings*, 'Facing the sun, untalkative, out of reach'. He has moved by train through an industrialised landscape, past suburban countryside toward 'Isolate villages, where removed lives / Loneliness clarifies', and still further to a place where he stands on a solitary shore. He has observed the society of getting and spending, the lives of those who 'Push through plate-glass swing doors to their desires', and he chooses to base his own psychological health on the freedom which is suggested to him by the expanse of the literal universe. The sky elicits from him a feeling of freedom and self-possession. 'Here' ends with a flight to pure contemplation which embodies Larkin's most overlooked kind of poetic effect:

> Here silence stands
> Like heat. Here leaves unnoticed thicken,
> Hidden weeds flower, neglected waters quicken,
> Luminously-peopled air ascends;
> And past the poppies bluish neutral distance
> Ends the land suddenly beyond a beach
> Of shapes and shingle. Here is unfenced existence:
> Facing the sun, untalkative, out of reach.

(WW, p. 9)

The disposition of the speaker at the end of the poem is one of solitary wonder. In the 'bluish neutral distance' he finds, as does the speaker contemplating the 'deep blue air' in 'High Windows', a spiritual liberation which follows his pondering the magnitude of the universe, a universe which is infinitely suggestive of freedom, just as it is also guarantor of the inviolable mystery of the self. Larkin has recently said that 'One longs for infinity and absence, the beauty of somewhere you're not',[7] and this obvious hunger in his work is visible in poems such as the above, just as it gives some credibility to Barbara Everett's suggestion that Larkin is a Symbolist poet who is concerned to suggest an infinite reality beyond the finite.[8] Yet we do not have to go past the example of D. H. Lawrence to see that the 'bluish neutral distance' is both English and carefully elemental as much as it is Symbolist. It represents the extent to which Larkin will limit his observing consciousness as a poet of passing wonder. He is not a poet who is confident of an absolute beyond.

The same poet who places the speaker in 'Here' in a climactic and final locus of facing the sun has the more ironic speaker in 'Dockery and Son' recoil from the confinement of Dockery's neatly settled life of marriage, social position and apparent success. After leaving Dockery in Oxford, he takes a train – a highly suggestive natural symbol of his own imaginative life – and falls asleep between Oxford and Sheffield. When he awakens, there is a symbolic connection quite casually made between himself and the 'Unhindered moon':

> I fell asleep, waking at the fumes
> And furnace-glares of Sheffield, where I changed,
> And ate an awful pie, and walked along
> The platform to its end to see the ranged
> Joining and parting lines reflect a strong
>
> Unhindered moon.
>
> (*WW*, p. 37)

The presence of the moon as 'strong' and as reflecting a travelling visage on the rails stands above the poem's other considerations as liberating, attractive to the speaker. Much later, in 'Vers de Société', we find this persona again, dreading the prospect of a dinner party and preferring instead to stay alone in the presence of the night sky, recharging his spirit with something more than prattle. He ultimately relinquishes his hermitage, changes his mind after gestures of self-mockery, but not until he has made his case for the value of solitude:

> Just think of all the spare time that has flown
>
> Straight into nothingness by being filled
> With forks and faces, rather than repaid
> Under a lamp, hearing the noise of the wind,
> And looking out to see the moon thinned
> To an air-sharpened blade.
>
> (*HW*, p. 35)

The sky is evoked with all of the freshness of a living presence and mystery, one that recalls Lawrence's similar conversations with the heavens. In one of the many instances in which Lawrence dealt with the value of solitary wonder, his poem 'Delight of Being Alone', he also invoked the sustaining example of the moon:

> I know no greater delight than the sheer delight of being alone.
> It makes me realise the delicious pleasure of the moon
> that she has in travelling by herself: throughout time,
> or the splendid growing of the ash-tree
> alone, on a hill-side in the north, humming in the wind.[9]

Lawrence and Larkin share a jealous concern for their solitude, a conviction that it is vital to their self-possession and indispensible to their predilection for wonder. In poem xix of *The North Ship* the speaker decides that he will 'attend to the trees and their gracious silence, / To winds that move' (*NS*, p. 31), and in 'Night Music' there is a valuing of the stars 'in their blazing solitude' (*NS*, p. 23). Solitude is the necessary disposition of the artist, in some ways, and in 'Reasons for Attendance', a poem about the choice between bachelorhood and marriage ('Surely, to think the lion's share / Of happiness is found by couples – sheer / Inaccuracy, as far as I'm concerned'), what calls the speaker, in the end, is not the music of the dance hall but the 'rough-tongued bell / (Art, if you like) whose individual sound / Insists I too am an individual' (*LD*, p. 18).

There is argument for the claim that Larkin's loneliness as a poet is connected with his regard for Hardy's poetry of solitary contemplation, but the fine detail of what occurs in Larkin's poems of contemplation brings the example of Lawrence more typically in view.[10] Larkin sees a positive value in loneliness and it has its basis in that kind of defence Lawrence more elaborately made for solitude in *Lady Chatterley's Lover* (1928) and in such poems as 'Delight of Being Alone' and 'The Uprooted'. The latter piece insists,

> People who complain of loneliness must have lost something,
> lost some living connection with the cosmos, out of themselves,
> lost their life-flow
> like a plant whose roots are cut.
> And they are crying like plants whose roots are cut.
> But the presence of other people will not give them new, rooted
>   connection
> it will only make them forget.
> The thing to do is in solitude slowly and painfully put forth new
>   roots
> into the unknown, and take root by oneself.[11]

There is nothing in Larkin as periphrastic as this, but it is notably an important concept in Lawrence which is stated here. Many of Larkin's poems struggle toward a beauty in their solitude and do so in widened settings which include a graphic picturing of the elemental world.

All of Larkin's volumes contain sensitive nature poems, ones in which the speaker is sometimes surprised by his sudden joy next to natural beauty. In 'Coming', the song of a thrush in early spring, 'Astonishing the brickwork', sets the scene where a tired speaker is moved to

> Feel like a child
> Who comes on a scene
> Of adult reconciling,
> And can understand nothing
> But the unusual laughter,
> And starts to be happy.

> (*LD*, p. 17)

And in 'Absences', another nature poem in *The Less Deceived*, in a scene of elemental beauty where 'Rain patters on a sea that tilts and sighs', the zestful contemplation of a stormy seascape finishes with the healing shout of cleansing joy: 'Such attics cleared of me! Such absences!' (*LD*, p. 40). So it should not be surprising that *High Windows* is a volume in which nature appears as a mysterious and beckoning presence which offers a refreshing purity in the sanity of its visage.

High Windows is Larkin's most Lawrentian volume. A number of its poems are sensitively alert in their contemplation of the natural world, and there is a freshness in their imagery, an engaging clarity. This is particularly true of many of the shorter pieces, but is also involved in that longest poem in the volume, 'Livings', a triptych in which the world of books, the world of commerce and the world of poetic imagination are evoked and implicitly compared. 'Livings' ends with the crisp imagery of the following lines;

> The bells discuss the hour's gradations,
> Dusty shelves hold prayers and proofs:
> Above, the Chaldean constellations
> Sparkle over crowded roofs.

> (*HW*, p. 15)

The elemental world is pictorially evoked in each section of the poem and is made the reference point from which the various lives or 'livings' are measured. The 'Sparkle' of the skyscape, its sharp beauty and expansiveness, appears suddenly at the close of section III as an implied comment on the confined and bookish life of a university don, a confinement which is also echoed in the very tight metrical pattern of the poem. On the other hand, the lightkeeper's life portrayed in section II looms above the other lives as a normative one, and the section introduces greater flexibility of rhythm and syntax. The lightkeeper–poet is solitary, but his aloofness renders him awake to the mysterious presence of the elemental world, its beauty and its energy:

> Seventy feet down
> The sea explodes upwards,
> Relapsing, to slaver
> Off landing-stage steps –
> Running suds, rejoice!
>
> Rocks writhe back to sight.
> Mussels, limpets,
> Husband their tenacity
> In the freezing slither –
> Creatures, I cherish you!
>
> By day, sky builds
> Grape-dark over the salt
> Unsown stirring fields.
> Radio rubs its legs,
> Telling me of elsewhere.

> (*HW*, p. 14)

The five stanzas of this section mimic the height of the lighthouse itself in their short line widths and free verse structure. The lyric energy of the piece – its strong verbs and exclamatory tone aiding its effectiveness – grows from an affirmation of the beauty and mystery of the elements in which the lightkeeper–poet lives.

Nature is more 'living' in *High Windows* than in Larkin's other volumes; it is more the measure of the human spirit, and more intimately conversant with the speakers in its shorter poems. 'Sad Steps', 'Cut Grass', 'The Trees', and 'Solar' are the poems which centrally express a desire for connection with the elemental, and we have already viewed its presence in 'Vers de Société'. 'Sad Steps' echoes and transforms Sir Philip Sidney's sonnet and revitalises it with an observing freshness in the imagery. Its tonal sadness and sarcasm renders it entirely Larkin's creation, and its solitary contemplation in the setting of a stark elemental beauty brings Lawrence again to mind:

> Groping back to bed after a piss
> I part thick curtains, and am startled by
> The rapid clouds, the moon's cleanliness.
>
> Four o'clock: wedge-shadowed gardens lie
> Under a cavernous, a wind-picked sky.
> There's something laughable about this,
>
> The way the moon dashes through clouds that blow
> Loosely as cannon-smoke to stand apart
> (Stone-coloured light sharpening the roofs below)
>
> High and preposterous and separate –
> Lozenge of love! Medallion of art!
> O wolves of memory! Immensements! No,
>
> One shivers slightly, looking up there.
> The hardness and the brightness and the plain
> Far-reaching singleness of that wide stare
>
> Is a reminder of the strength and pain
> Of being young; that it can't come again,
> But is for others undiminished somewhere.

(HW, p. 32)

The cleverness at the outset, its mixture of the beautiful image with a manner of ridicule, is recognisable as Larkin's penchant for self-mockery and his habit of restraining the flight of wonder from soaring past the bounds of transient awe. 'Sad Steps' states an irony and a beauty at once; it is true and beautiful in the mixture common to Larkin's romantic poetry, and its irreverence saves it from being solemn and unconvincing.

A beauty is captured in the physical clarity of the moon as made present in 'The rapid clouds, the moon's cleanliness', and in the 'hardness and brightness and the plain / Far-reaching singleness of that wide stare'. The spiritual potential of the moment is openly stated in the speaker's claim to be 'startled' by the beauty, and in the shudder of recognition given in the line, 'One shivers slightly, looking up there' – even though this is a shiver which also lyrically states his chagrin about transience, failure and old age. The passing quality of the wonder is intimately connected to his recognition that the moon is losing symbolic meaning for him; nevertheless, it is in the peeling-away of the symbolic epithets that its significance, its clear purity is found.

The aging speaker is identified as a sceptical and a romantic figure at the same time. He is gracious in spite of his obvious disquiet and sadness. In recognising his own failing composure, he is not jealous of other significances to the moon, especially as 'Lozenge of love', so he can bow from the scene with some dignity. The moment of awareness gives him a tenuous stay against despair and a retrieved self-possession which maturely moves outward as a gesture of goodwill toward the young. In the playful irony, sceptical realism, pleasure in beauty and in the ability for praise, 'Sad Steps' draws on all aspects of Larkin's poetic personality for its rightness; the contemplative centre of its setting is one in which life is measured against the universe seen as mysterious.

Lawrence claimed that it is in these momentary realisations in 'pure relationship' with the 'living universe about us'[12] that major art reaches its fullest and almost religious intensity, and he constantly stressed the sanity of attuning the imagination to the cycles of nature, its natural events and ritual. Such a concern for cycle is also emphatic in *High Windows*. In 'Forget What Did' the sad and tired speaker thinks back over his 'opaque childhood' in gestures of regret; but absorption in sadness is resisted as he moves toward a statement of purpose. He resolves that, if the future pages of his diary are filled, it will be with 'observed / Celestial recurrences, / The day the flowers come, / And when the birds go' (*HW*, p. 16). Lawrence once listed these observed intimacies as including 'me and the trees or flowers, me and the earth, me and the skies and sun and stars, me and the moon: an infinity of pure relations, big and little, like the stars of the sky'.[13] The observed 'recurrences' in *High Windows* range throughout that list of Lawrence's, and in some of the poems encourage hope, in the form of a momentary peace which assuages a tendency toward gloom.

In 'The Trees', for example, a moment of 'pure relationship' is accomplished in spite of a threatening undertone of despondency. The poem is amenable to Lawrence's diction about cycles, and it enacts Larkin's own new interest in 'recurrences':

> The trees are coming into leaf
> Like something almost being said;
> The recent buds relax and spread,
> Their greenness is a kind of grief.
>
> Is it that they are born again
> And we grow old? No, they die too.
> Their yearly trick of looking new
> Is written down in rings of grain.
>
> Yet still the unresting castles thresh
> In fullgrown thickness every May.
> Last year is dead, they seem to say,
> Begin afresh, afresh, afresh.

> (*HW*, p. 12)

The lyric base of 'The Trees' is one of praise in spite of the threat of a countervailing sadness of tone. The sadness and the cleverness unite in the creation of a registered moment of communion which is also left open rather than used as a substance through which to state a myth. As in 'Cut Grass', a similarly framed piece, the contemplation is one in which the observer and the observed merge in the momentary recognition of a living relationship. The almost cosmic sense of pain suggested in the comment that 'Their greenness is a kind of grief' is diminished by the humour which urbanely refers to the ritual as a 'yearly trick of looking new'. Any inclination to destroy the appreciation of cycle with ironic quibble is overcome in the note of praise and connection which closes the poem. The last stanza well states the 'fullgrown thickness' of the trees, and the speaker participates in the mysterious cycle of renewal with his concluding and prayerful repetition, 'Begin afresh, afresh, afresh'.

Central to Lawrence's appreciation of these moments of relatedness, such as we experience in 'Sad Steps' and 'The Trees', was his conviction that they can issue a healing-effect, can accumulate into the basis of an imaginative health or living wisdom. 'What we want is to destroy our false, inorganic connections,' he famously asserted, 'especially those related to money, and re-establish the living organic connections, with the cosmos, the sun and earth, with mankind and nation and family. Start with the sun, and the rest will slowly, slowly happen.'[14] It is worth turning from the close of 'The Trees' to 'Solar' with these words of Lawrence's in mind. 'Solar' is here quoted in full:

> Suspended lion face
> Spilling at the centre
> Of an unfurnished sky
> How still you stand,
> And how unaided
> Single stalkless flower
> You pour unrecompensed.
>
> The eye sees you
> Simplified by distance
> Into an origin,
> Your petalled head of flames
> Continuously exploding.
> Heat is the echo of your
> Gold.
>
> Coined there among
> Lonely horizontals
> You exist openly.
> Our needs hourly
> Climb and return like angels.
> Unclosing like a hand,
> You give for ever.

(*HW*, p. 33)

'Solar' is Lawrentian in its valuing of the mysterious presence of the sun. Yet it is distinctly Larkin's creation in the quiet reserve of its tone and its unmistakable sense of spiritual woundedness. The craft of the poem is sharply pictorial; the sun is seen as 'lion face', 'stalkless flower, Gold', and as 'Unclosing like a hand', all images which rush into and complement one another. Each formal detail of 'Solar' nourishes the thematic expression of the sun's essence as the natural symbol of perfection in the universe, the centre of all creation. Even the phonetic level of the form, its layering of *o* sounds, mimes the circularity and perfection which the images suggest. The speaker resists any flight to mythic conviction with the inclusion of the phrase, 'The eye sees you / Simplified by distance / Into an origin'. The wonder, that is, is checked by the speaker's reserve without that reserve destroying the beauty. He refuses, in Lawrence's diction, to 'nail it down' into a myth. Nevertheless, the groundtone of praise is sustained: the poet does not unmask the face of God, yet he is rewarded in his beholding openness and reveals a moment of presence which is tissued with mystery.

Lawrence wrote in 'Aristocracy' that man's life

> consists in a relation with all things: stone, earth, trees, flowers, water, insects, fishes, birds, creatures, sun, rainbow, children, women, other men. But his greatest and final relation is with the sun, the sun of suns: and with the night, which is moon and dark and stars. In the last great connections, he lifts his body speechless to the sun, and, the same body, but so different, to the moon and the stars, and the open spaces between the stars.[15]

With that assertion in mind, one is provoked to notice anew the important but quiet presence of the sun in Larkin's major volumes.

The sun appears in Larkin's world as benevolent and mysterious and as the signification of a dignity to life and a hope. We see it in 'Here' and in 'Solar'. In 'The Old Fools' it appears as the 'sun's / Faint friendliness on the wall some lonely / Rain-ceased midsummer evening' (*HW*, p. 20). 'The Whitsun Weddings' looks toward 'London spread out in the sun, / Its postal districts packed like squares of wheat' (*WW*, p. 23), and in 'The Explosion' the colliers are imagined by their wives as 'Gold as on coin, walking / Somehow from the sun towards them' (*HW*, p. 42), like Lawrence's aristocrats of the sun. And there are many other instances, but rising above all others is the image of the sunlight which glitters mysteriously in 'Water':

> If I were called in
> To construct a religion
> I should make use of water.
>
> Going to church
> Would entail a fording
> To dry, different clothes;
>
> My liturgy would employ
> Images of sousing,
> A furious devout drench,
>
> And I should raise in the east
> A glass of water
> Where any-angled light
> Would congregate endlessly.

(*WW*, p. 20)

The religion is one of mystery, a substitute 'construct' in which the elements enjoy a major role. The play of the sun on water intimates a sense of the mystery of the living world and also approximates Lawrence's rainbow imagery. It as well picks up the 'miracle of glass' (*NS*, p. 13) referred to in poem II in *The North Ship*. As an undefined hope it brings to mind Lawrence's rainbow at the close of *The Rainbow*. There, Ursula Brangwen moves spiritually above the 'brittle corruption of houses and factories' (Lawrence's equivalent to Larkin's 'cobble-close families / In mill-towns on dark mornings' – *WW*, p. 11), and she is aided in her move above pessimism by the saving beauty and wonder she finds in the material world:

And the rainbow stood on the earth. She knew that the sordid people who crept hard-scaled and separate on the face of the world's corruption were living still, that the rainbow was arched in their blood and would quiver to life in their spirit, that they would cast off their horny covering of disintegration, that the new, clean, naked bodies would issue to a new germination, to a new growth, rising to the light and the wind and the clean rain of heaven.[16]

It is not precisely, however, in the figure of Ursula that we find a character who is in personal kinship with Larkin's wondrous persona. Thinking about the sadness, anxieties and chagrin about transience and death which remain in Larkin's persona, Tom Brangwen is the character in *The Rainbow* who more thoroughly comes to mind. In *The Rainbow*, it is Tom who is sad, aging, always torn between hope and bitterness; and it is Tom who incessantly explores the artistic and religious traces of order that surround him in his daily life. He has things in common with Larkin's speaker in 'Church Going' and in 'High Windows', in that he is attentive to the beauty of both nature and the architectural world. He is solitary and also hungry for a sense of beauty and atonement. At Anna's wedding he drifts into a state of reverie in which he considers his failures and his age. At that point his mind is compelled by the 'blue window at the back of the altar'. The ensuing moment of wonder mitigates his sense of disenchantment and reinvigorates his being with a spontaneous hope:

> How did one grow old – how could one become confident? He wished he felt older. Why, what difference was there, as far as he felt matured or completed, between him now and him at his wedding? He felt himself tiny, a little, upright figure on a plain circled round with the immense, roaring sky. . . . When did one come to an end? There was no end, no finish, only this vast roaring space . . . that was the clue. He exulted strangely, with torture. He would go on with his wife, he and she like two children camping on the plains. What was sure but the endless sky? But it was so sure, so boundless.
>   Still the royal blue colour burned and blazed and sported itself in the web of darkness before him, unwearingly rich and splendid. . . . Always it was so unfinished and unformed.[17]

It is the tension of Tom's personality which gives to his sensibility a kinship with Larkin's struggle with pessimism. As a consciousness which is both 'less deceived' and romantic at the same time, Tom reflects Lawrence's own tendency toward despair and also his unwillingness to give in to that despair because of his durable sense of beauty and his final regard for the mystery of existence. And if it is at all possible to say that there is a complete vision in Larkin's volumes, it takes the shape of just such a precarious dialectic. Larkin is a poet who continually turns up moments of grave doubt in his chronicle, but these doubts are constantly qualified by his romantic impulse, his capacity for surprise at the beauty of the world.

In the 'Earth' section of 'Transformations', Lawrence was to say that 'on me lies the duty / To see you all, sordid or radiant tissued'.[18] That comment is in keeping with similar statements made by Larkin's other major mentors, Dr Johnson and Thomas Hardy. Johnson's Imlac stated that 'To the poet nothing can be useless. Whatever is beautiful, and whatever is dreadful, must be familiar to his imagination.'[19] And Hardy once asserted that, 'if way to the Better there be, it exacts a full look at the Worst'.[20] Lawrence, Johnson and Hardy all share with Larkin a conviction that literature must deal with the failing aspects of the human condition as much as with its mystery and beauty. None the less, in their relative ability to enact such precepts there are radical differences between these writers in the effects they achieve. For neither Johnson nor Hardy seems capable of giving such full embodiment to the 'radiant tissued' aspect of reality as Lawrence is. It is from Lawrence that Larkin's 'other' dimension receives tutelage, and the result is the presence, in his chronicle, of rare moments of experiential surprise in which there is a self-conscious check on his gloom and a willingness to deflate his own tendency toward despair.

Moreover, Larkin's affinity with Lawrence does not end with a shared wonder at the sanity of the elemental world. It is there also in Larkin's poetry of ritual community events. Lawrence was as much concerned with the defeat of ordinary people by a commercial and materialistic culture as is Larkin. And in the place of that diminutive culture he sought to sustain the values of commonplace rituals and the spontaneous customs of ordinary life. The 'other' side of Larkin's Johnsonian analysis of contemporary culture brings much of Lawrence's wisdom in these matters into play. So the 'other' Larkin is not simply the solitary nature mystic; he is also a figure who finds an analogous sense of mystery in the commonplace life he beholds. There is a fragile wonder in Larkin's more positive poetry of social perspective, and it gives a further credibility, I think, to the value of his cleansing social scepticism. It is in his poetry of ritual community events that we most fulsomely witness what it is in the name of that his more satirical social poetry takes aim. It takes aim, we shall see, in the name of a Lawrentian series of values.

5   Family and Nation

When Larkin says, 'I don't want to transcend the commonplace, I love the commonplace life. Everyday things are lovely to me',[1] he speaks from the more positive aspect of his identity as a poet of social reality. Moreover, the comment captions quite effectively those poems in his chronicle which sing of the beauty of community life, even as they also remain conscious of the 'greeds / And garbage' (*WW*, p. 22) he worries about as a possible metaphor for the future. Larkin finds a quiet hope in the lives of ordinary people, and it is there in his work as a function of both his compassion as a poet and his sensitivity to the mystery of the human being. It is indeed very striking that a poet who is commonly charged with being aloof and smug in his attitudes to life should contain in his vision a democracy of attention to the commonplace after all. Yet we have already seen his capacity for deflating his own initial gestures toward superiority, and a few of his poems comment harshly on social arrogance in others. Such poems are in a sense prefatory to Larkin's more buoyant concerns as a poet of ordinary beauty, and they include implicit statement of his own desire to achieve and write from a better self.

Battling social superiority, egotism of the simple kind, is central to many of Larkin's works; it is there in the quarrel with himself evidenced in dramatic lyrics such as 'Church Going' and 'High Windows', for example, where smugness is chipped away and left behind as an imaginative narrowness, as we have seen. There is a willingness on Larkin's part to be critical of his own tares and cranks, his knee-jerk habits, that is to say; so it makes sense that he should be satirical of those who promote themselves above ordinary humanity or the commonplace and therefore fail to recognise their own share in the prosaic world. I don't think Lawrence is directly involved in these particular poems, even though the absurdity he disparages in such poems as 'To be Superior' and 'The Oxford Voice' send forward, perhaps, a bit of an echo. When both Lawrence and Larkin look around them it is

77

the academic species of the snob that appears to them as being perhaps the worst of the lot.

At the jazz performance, in 'For Sidney Bechet', the mixed humanity of the audience includes 'scholars *manqués*' who 'nod around unnoticed / Wrapped up in personnels like old plaids' (*WW*, p. 16); and the solitary figure in 'Vers de Société' dreads the invitation to a dinner party partly because he does not want to participate in the narrow, ego-bound conversations ('Asking that ass about his fool research' – *HW*, p. 35). An American variety of 'fool research' and nodding around unnoticed is given to us in the figure of Jake Balokowsky in 'Posterity', who is cast (in concrete) as the poet's own biographer, a sort of Caliban careerist who wants to 'put this bastard on the skids' so he can get to work 'on Protest Theater' (*HW*, p. 27). Balokowsky has become a figure larger than the poem which places his glibness where it belongs, and I think is best left there next to the 'Coke dispenser', since the poem, unlike so many of Larkin's other works, does not build toward clearly positive values in the name of what it easily destroys. It is through the portraiture of another academic snob (who is more successful and probably smoother in public than Jake), the imaginatively limited character in 'Naturally the Foundation Will Bear your Expenses', that we witness Larkin's assertion of the value of the commonplace when considered next to the narrowness of assumed academic superiority:

> Hurrying to catch my Comet
>   One dark November day,
> Which soon would snatch me from it
>   To the sunshine of Bombay,
> I pondered pages Berkeley
>   Not three weeks since had heard,
> Perceiving Chatto darkly
>   Through the mirror of the Third.
>
> Crowds, colourless and careworn,
>   Have made my taxi late,
> Yet not till I was airborne
>   Did I recall the date –
> That day when Queen and Minister
>   And Band of Guards and all
> Still act their solemn-sinister
>   Wreath-rubbish in Whitehall.

It used to make me throw up,
   These mawkish nursery games:
O when will England grow up?
   – But I outsoar the Thames,
And dwindle off down Auster
   To greet Professor Lal
(He once met Morgan Forster),
   My contact and my pal.

(*WW*, p. 13)

The genteel crassness of the speaker in this satirical and inspired dramatic monologue is revealed in the crudity of his response to the 'Crowds, colourless and careworn' (a general image which Larkin makes into compassionate poetry in other of his works), his impatient reaction to what he considers the childishness of their attendance at the memorial ceremony. Ironically, while he considers himself to have transcended such 'solemn-sinister / Wreath-rubbish', his transcendence is a 'Hurrying to catch my Comet', or a physical freedom to 'outsoar the Thames' only; it is not in the least a spiritual, in any sense earned, superiority he embodies.

There is a devastating appropriateness to Larkin's revelation of the contradiction between the speaker's scorn for the conventional mentality of the crowd and his own, merely different, conventional bearing. While Larkin's own zest for language appears in incidental phrases, the bored and superior clichés of the speaker ('It used to make me throw up,/These mawkish . . .') and the cliché nature of his own behaviour – anger about underlings, annoyance at small inconveniences, recital of places visited and people known – are self-condemning and congruent with his practice of getting his opinions second hand, 'Through the mirror of the Third'. His lecture is a repeat performance wherever he goes – and it appears to be the only lecture he has. While he uses phrases of understanding such as 'Perceiving' and 'pondered', his self-deceived nature prevents him, ironically, from perceiving anything whatsoever about his own part in the concerns of humanity in the main.

It is the most blasting irony in the poem that it will be a 'foundation', after all, which will bear his expenses. The contempt he feels for the 'Crowds, colourless and careworn' leaves out the perception that foundations do such things as send his type 'To the sunshine of Bombay', where he can deliver his derivative lecture. Such callousness is in keeping with his careerist disrespect for most people in the poem, his 'contact and his pal' most especially. The lilting, nursery rhyme meter in the piece not only encases the thin sensibility of the speaker; it puts formally into perspective the disjunction between his view of the memorial service as 'mawkish nursery games' and the poet's engaged departure from the metrical norm that is given in the alliterative line about the careworn crowds. The thin sarcasm is in the speaker; the compassion is in the poem's more flexible form and vision.

No doubt some will think that Larkin makes heavy weather with such unimaginative and insensitive types. But we have at this stage a reasonably thorough sense of the poet's concern with the pathos of those crowds, a pathos which includes a realisation of their identity as victimised ordinary humanity. Moreover, there is something very positive in the memorial service which the poet wishes to value. The service is a ritual community event which brings into organic being a community's set of serious thoughts about death and humanity. Traditional life, in an odd way, survives in the service, corny as the superior-minded speaker might find it. And, in his more buoyant poetry about ritual community life, Larkin values very highly a spiritual health which is inseparable from an appreciation of the interrelatedness of the self with common humanity. This idea allies Larkin's poetry with that of Romantic poets such as Wordsworth, but the finer detail of its enactment brings D. H. Lawrence again into central view.

In *Apocalypse* (1931) Lawrence advocated the health of remaining spiritually awake to the 'living organic connections' with the universe which we have seen Larkin turn into a poetry of temporary wonder in his more elemental and solitary poems. And Lawrence went further in his concern with these 'connections', including the important connection with humanity:

> My soul knows that I am part of the human race, my soul is an organic part of the great human soul, as my spirit is part of my nation. In my own very self, I am part of my family. There is nothing of me that is alone except my mind, and we shall find that the mind has no existence by itself, it is only the glitter of the sun on the surface of the waters.

So my individualism is really an illusion. I am a part of the great whole, and can never escape. But I *can* deny my connections, break them, and become a fragment. Then I am wretched.[2]

Lawrence and Larkin insist on the value of their solitude, their aloneness ('Beyond all this, the wish to be alone' – *LD*, p. 22), and at the same time have written works which connect with humanity in this organic and engaged way at the level of art. The sensitivity to mystery that is nourished by their solitude often moves outward to an appreciation of a social beauty that is the more perceptible when they attend to community life in its moments of spontaneous ceremony.

Lawrence's talent for writing an art of social ritual is perhaps most prized in *The Rainbow*, and it is in Larkin's three major poems about the ordinary beauty of festival events that we witness his shared conviction with Lawrence that 'my spirit is part of my nation'. In 'The Whitsun Weddings', 'To the Sea' and 'Show Saturday' Larkin steps past the inhibiting aspects of his posture as a 'less deceived', ironic realist, and writes a poetry of festival community events. These poems participate in the spontaneous meaning of humanity and their speakers grow to realise that they are 'part of a whole', that there is an otherness to which they belong. These are dominantly celebratory works of art but they do not entirely erase Larkin's concerns as a poet of social satire. In a secondary manner, his concerns as a poet of the contemporary commercial wasteland are included as a measure of realism in their shape. Their positive dimension lies in the success with which they state the 'other' Larkin. In their revelation of moments of 'living organic connection' with humanity, they lift the poet momentarily above his dejection.

'The Whitsun Weddings' is structured in a fashion which recalls 'Church Going' in the care it takes to educate an initially detached speaker away from the inept wryness of his established personality toward a further seriousness which releases his capacity for praise. The figure speaking in 'The Whitsun Weddings' is presented to us as the least likely of narrators to appreciate the festivity of the events which slowly intrude on his detachment. The first two stanzas introduce us to his laconic bearing as we overhear his ponderings about the industrialised landscape the train passes through. The train carries its passengers through the visual squalor of one, as witness 'the next town, new and nondescript, / Approached with acres of dismantled cars' (*WW*, p. 21). It is only later, after the contrary imagery which closes the poem, that we look back to these early stanzas and regard them as a picture of the unpromising (and negative) Eden in which the weddings take place.

The three middle stanzas re-create a growing interest in the speaker, a burgeoning curiosity about the rumble and gaiety of the weddings. 'At first, I didn't notice what noise / The weddings made', he says at the beginning of the third stanza. Yet in the next he is on the edge of his seat: 'Struck, I leant / More promptly out next time, more curiously, / And I saw it all again in different terms' (*WW*, p. 21). It is at this point that we discern the deeper personality of the figure, and the 'different terms' are the result of his ability, for all of his detachment, to look at things 'more curiously'. A surface posture of inhibited irony is peeled away, thrown aside as beside the point. By the end of the fifth stanza there is a new openness of disposition in the speaker and he is moving toward spontaneous participation in the small beauty of the festivities:

> We passed them, grinning and pomaded, girls
> In parodies of fashion, heels and veils,
> All posed irresolutely, watching us go,
>
> As if out on the end of an event
>   Waving goodbye
> To something that survived it. Struck, I leant
> More promptly out next time, more curiously,
> And saw it all again in different terms:
> The fathers with broad belts under their suits
> And seamy foreheads: mothers loud and fat;
> An uncle shouting smut; and then the perms,
> The nylon gloves and jewellery-substitutes,
> The lemons, mauves, and olive-ochres that
>
> Marked off the girls unreally from the rest.
>   Yes, from cafés
> And banquet-halls up yards, and bunting-dressed
> Coach-party annexes, the wedding-days
> Were coming to an end. All down the line

Fresh couples climbed aboard: the rest stood round;
The last confetti and advice were thrown,
And, as we moved, each face seemed to define
Just what it saw departing: children frowned
At something dull; fathers had never known

Success so huge and farcical. . . .

(*WW*, pp. 21–2)

The felt life of the scenes, their visage as confusion and awkward beauty, is dramatised in the breathless syntax. That syntax carries the speaker's sympathy with the events and is the vehicle of intimate images of family relationships and embarrassed excitement. It includes the speaker ('we moved') as a part of the event, and in that participation he moves past his earlier bored self to a moment of 'living relationship'. Unlike the traveller in 'Naturally the Foundation Will Bear your Expenses', he finds a connection with common humanity and he celebrates it.

Larkin's gift for noticing and re-creating human gestures is manifest in the telling symbolic yawns and grins, and Lawrence's novelistic example is present here, I think, as a technical affinity. The crowded gaiety of these middle stanzas bears comparison with the similarly populous joy whose life we are invited to view in the 'Wedding at the Marsh' chapter of *The Rainbow*. As Lawrence describes it, 'It was a beautiful sunny day for the wedding, a muddy earth but a bright sky', and the wedding-party gathers at the Brangwen house as an excited crowd:

There was a great bustle. The front door is opened, and the wedding guests are walking down the garden path, whilst those still waiting peer through the window, and the little crowd at the gate gorps and stretches. How funny such dressed-up people look in the winter sunshine!

They are gone – another lot! There begins to be more room. Anna comes down blushing and very shy, to be viewed in her white silk and her veil. Her mother-in-law surveys her objectively, twitches the white train, arranges the folds of the veil and asserts herself.

Loud exclamations from the window that the bridegroom's carriage has just passed.

'Where's your hat, father, and your gloves?' cries the bride, stamping her white slipper, her eyes flashing through her veil. He hunts round – his hair is ruffled. Everybody has gone but the bride and her father. He is ready – his face very red and daunted. Tilly dithers in the little porch, waiting to open the door. A waiting woman walks round Anna, who asks:

'Am I all right?'

She is ready. She bridles herself and looks queenly. She waves her hand sharply to her father:

'Come here!'

He goes. She puts her hand very slightly on his arm, and holding her bouquet like a shower, stepping oh very graciously, just a little impatient with her father for being so red in the face, she sweeps slowly past the fluttering Tilly, and down the path. There are hoarse shouts at the gate, and all her floating foamy whiteness passes slowly into the cab.[3]

The friends and relatives are all viewed as a tumble of humanity by Lawrence here; they are excited, partly shy, some are half tipsy and all are full of awkward gestures and sometimes lewd comments, just as they are in the middle stanzas of Larkin's poem. Larkin has modestly stated that in the creation of 'The Whitsun Weddings' there was little he had to do, that 'It was just the transcription of a very happy afternoon. I didn't change a thing, it was just there to be written down',[4] and there is a convincing realism in the poem which helps to underwrite his claim. Yet the proximity of his celebratory air to Lawrence's, an unmistakable generosity of observation, is so close to Lawrence's *Rainbow* chapter that it is obvious, I think, that it is with Lawrence's immediacy of wonder that Larkin gives internal coherence to his moment of living relationship. Both writers participate in the innocent chaos and beauty of the festivities.

As 'The Whitsun Weddings' moves to its celebratory finale it gathers in its experience of living connection and moves the meaning of the day toward a moment of transcendence. The concluding stanza is designed, nevertheless, with that ambiguity common to Larkin's moments of wonder in that it celebrates the heightened moment without building it into an absolute. To recall Hulme's words on classical moments of flight, it stays 'mixed up with earth' as a way of keeping the measure of the meaning realistic. The descending lines of 'The Whitsun Weddings' are also ascending ones; they measure the found beauty in a tone of hopefulness that is also tinged with apprehension. There is a prizing of the 'frail / Travelling coincidence', the moment of connection, and there is an implicit statement that it is a fragile moment as well, since the couples are moving toward the 'postal districts' of London. The imagery of the stanza is fertile, but that the couples' destination is the locus of the poet's other concerns as a social poet brings into play, of course, his reservations about contemporary dreams of fulfilment.

In the strange feeling of comingled love, celebration and fear which the last stanza creates, 'The Whitsun Weddings' shares an affinity with Lawrence's poem 'Tommies in the Train'. Lawrence's poem is specifically like 'The Whitsun Weddings' on a series of counts: both poems are set on a train; the sun is evoked at the beginning as mysterious presence; their evocations are of a bearing of beauty and innocence in the passengers; and the moments of awareness that 'my spirit is part of my nation' are torn away from the narrators as the trains head for their destinations with reality in the end. There are so many likenesses that the two poems are placed in conversation. 'Tommies in the Train' is here quoted in full:

> The sun shines,
> The coltsfoot flowers along the railway banks
> Shine like a flat coin which Jove in thanks
> Strews each side the lines.
>
> A steeple
> In purple elms, daffodils
> Sparkle beneath, luminous hills
> Beyond – and no people.
>
> England, O Danaë
> To this spring of cosmic gold
> That falls on your lap of mould! –
> What then are we?
>
> What are we
> Clay-coloured, who roll in fatigue,
> As the train falls league after league
> From our destiny?

A hand is over my face,
A cold hand. – I peep between the fingers
To watch the world that lingers
Behind, yet keeps pace.

Always there, as I peep
Between the fingers that cover my face!
Which then is it that falls from its place
And rolls down the steep?

Is it the train
That falls like a meteorite
Backward into space, to alight
Never again?

Or is it the illusory world
That falls from reality
As we look? Or are we
Like a thunderbolt hurled?

One or another
Is lost, since we fall apart
Endlessly, in one motion depart
From each other.[5]

In Lawrence's poem there is the registration of the observer's momentary connection with the humanity of his nation, a rendering which is cast as an experience of pathos and beauty at once. The illusion of selfhood which he speaks of in *Apocalypse* disappears. There is a regard for the beauty of the day and the innocence in the passengers which is valued the more because of the feeling that it is threatened by the experience (of the war) which marks the times, and to which the tommies are headed.

Larkin's closing lines in 'The Whitsun Weddings' are more compact and different in stanzaic pattern, but the vorticistic effect of the imagery is similar:

I thought of London spread out in the sun,
Its postal districts packed like squares of wheat:

There we were aimed. And as we raced across
   Bright knots of rail
Past standing Pullmans, walls of blackened moss
Came close, and it was nearly done, this frail
Travelling coincidence; and what it held
Stood ready to be loosed with all the power
That being changed can give. We slowed again,
And as the tightened brakes took hold, there swelled
A sense of falling, like an arrow-shower
Sent out of sight, somewhere becoming rain.

(*WW*, p. 23)

In both poems there is a re-creation of an exceptionally heightened moment of connection with 'family and nation', but Larkin's is understandably the more celebratory piece because of its context of festivity. As a result, the 'meteorite' of Lawrence's poem is lifted upward to become an 'arrow-shower' in Larkin's text, and it is one which is fertile, 'somewhere becoming rain', and therefore a more hopeful metaphor than Lawrence's. Each poem praises a mixed quality of beauty, innocence and pathos in its representation of observed humanity, and each also records a fear that the moment of appreciation is transitory and threatened. The relationships between observers and observed can only be stated in all of their ambiguity by a rushing imagery which includes motion, connection and fear; and this is dramatised in each case as the experience of intimate witness and anxious feeling at once. Each poem embodies a moment in which the mystery of human *being* and meaning is prized and recorded with a loving and compassionate glance. 'The Whitsun Weddings' is both beautiful and true at the same time; it values the 'living organic connection' and remains realistic in its recognition of the rarity of the moment and how its exceptional meaning is bracketed by the squalid landscape evoked at the beginning of the poem, and by the confinement of the suburban reality toward which the couples travel.

'The Whitsun Weddings' is a magnificent social poem, one of a beauty and praise which transcends the junk-ridden nature of contemporary reality and yet keeps its abstractions away from absolutes and conclusions. Larkin remains content to celebrate the feeling of grace which surfaces from observed ordinary life, and keeps his meaning close to the level of intimate participation in the festive events. And what we, as readers, witness in this poem is thought as experience, thought as living reality and not as dry idea. In 'Thought' Lawrence says, 'Thought is gazing on to the face of life, and reading what can be read', and he also concludes that poem with the suggestion that 'Thought is a man in his wholeness wholly attending.'[6] The meaning, that is to say, is in the sensitive alertness rather than in a series of abstractions, and the poet's and the reader's reward alike is in the potential for appreciation of beauty and connection of that order Lawrence so eloquently describes in *Apocalypse*.

Larkin's ability for celebrating the beauty of human community is more recently represented in *High Windows* by 'To the Sea' and 'Show Saturday'. These two poems share with the earlier 'Whitsun Weddings' a respectful sense of the 'great human soul' as quietly perceptible to that consciousness which can move past irony to a 'wholeness wholly attending'. 'To the Sea' is a very successful poem in this regard and the poet has perhaps sensed this, given that he places it as the opening poem in the volume. 'To the Sea' re-creates a casual moment of 'living organic connection' that the speaker shares with both the human and the natural world:

> To step over the low wall that divides
> Road from concrete walk above the shore
> Brings sharply back something known long before –
> The miniature gaiety of seasides.
> Everything crowds under the low horizon:
> Steep beach, blue water, towels, red bathing caps,
> The small hushed waves' repeated fresh collapse
> Up the warm yellow sand, and further off
> A white steamer stuck in the afternoon –
>
> Still going on, all of it, still going on!
> To lie, eat, sleep in hearing of the surf
> (Ears to transistors, that sound tame enough
> Under the sky), or gently up and down
> Lead the uncertain children, frilled in white
> And grasping at enormous air, or wheel
> The rigid old along for them to feel
> A final summer, plainly still occurs
> As half an annual pleasure, half a rite,

As when, happy at being on my own,
I searched the sand for Famous Cricketers
Or, farther back, my parents, listeners
To the same seaside quack, first became known.
Strange to it now, I watch the cloudless scene:
To the same clear water over smoothed pebbles,
The distant bathers' weak protesting trebles
Down at its edge, and then the cheap cigars,
The chocolate-papers, tea-leaves, and, between

The rocks, the rusting soup-tins, till the first
Few families start the trek back to the cars.
The white steamer has gone. Like breathed-on glass
The sunlight has turned milky. If the worst
Of flawless weather is our falling short,
It may be that through habit these do best,
Coming to water clumsily undressed
Yearly; teaching their children by a sort
Of clowning; helping the old, too, as they ought.

(*HW*, pp. 9–10)

As in the visually accumulating stanzas of 'The Whitsun
Weddings', there is an observed particularity that guarantees the
living connection the poet feels with his surrounding world, and it
is a world that includes 'family and nation' in a totally
unconscious and ritualistic unity. The attending observation is
one of communion, and the unity includes the beach, the sky, the
people, their funny junk and the poet, all at once. 'To the Sea'
enacts the totality of connections Lawrence listed in *Apocalypse* as
including both the natural and the human worlds. The 'miniature
gaiety' of the scene is recorded as a vision which collects all small
details into a praise of ordinariness, just as it also hints at a 'living
organic connection' which the crowd quite unconsciously has
with the sea.

Larkin's instinct for praise in 'To the Sea' is not diminished by
irony; the humour in the poem is the humour of recognition, a
smiling respect for the small beauty of the people as made visible
in their moments of off-guardedness and spontaneity. All sense of
the commonplace beauty of the people is caught in generous
images of their gestures, not in abstractions about them. The

children are 'frilled in white / and grasping at enormous air', or they 'wheel / The rigid old along for them to feel / A final summer'. Each image of individual humanity, and of generational continuity, is an image of spontaneous unity to the 'wholly attending' observer. In spite of the intruding (and truthful) natural symbolism of the litter on the beach, the speaker is more interested in the spiritual weight of the event when seen as 'annual pleasure, half-rite'. The latent stimulus in the scene for a condemnation of social obesity is resisted in a respect for the quality of small mystery which momentarily transcends the congruent presence of squalor. The 'white steamer stuck in the afternoon' exists in the far distance of the observation as a suggestive embodiment of the potential art of the scene, the reality which approximates art as a found moment in which 'gazing at the face of life' is rewarded with a hint of deep meaning that is inseparable from the scene itself. The art is in the appreciation and in the skill with which the poet visually and tonally records his moment of participation in 'family and nation'.

In 'Show Saturday' Larkin's same impulse to praise and witness is stimulated by the event of an annual country fair. After a long listing of the plenitude of sights and sounds, he concludes his engaged observation in lines which read like a gloss on the social concerns of both 'To the Sea' and the earlier 'Whitsun Weddings'. 'Show Saturday' also includes a realistic reference to the values of the commercial wasteland familiar to us from his more satirical social poems. Speaking of the unparaphrasable power of the cyclical human event, he ends,

> Let it stay hidden there like strength, below
> Sale-bills and swindling; something people do,
> Not noticing how time's rolling smithy-smoke
> Shadows much greater gestures; something they share
> That breaks ancestrally each year into
> Regenerate union. Let it always be there.

> (*HW*, p. 39)

All three of these major social poems – Larkin's poems which deal with 'living organic connections' with family and nation – share with Lawrence's very similar concerns, an ability not only imaginatively to participate in the unity, but also to praise the beauty of the commonplace in spite of concerns about its frailty in the context of a commercial, otherwise lifeless, culture. Larkin and Lawrence each celebrate a positive value that transcends the reality of 'Sale-bills and swindling' which Larkin is more angrily attentive to in his satirical poems about the popular imagination.

'The Whitsun Weddings', 'To the Sea' and 'Show Saturday' best represent the more positive Larkin of social commentary, the poet who is inspired with a Lawrentian sense of the small beauty of the human being as seen in its moments of participation in ritual community events. This triptych of poems exists in Larkin's canon as profound modifier of the bleaker social vision we experience in his Johnsonian poems about society, poems which tend, on the whole, to be more toughly analytical, more attentive to the folly of human wishes, and less certain that any degree of beauty and ritual survives in the wasteland of contemporary culture. There is a dialectical rhythm to all of this, an openness to the variety of life, which is familiar in Larkin's other concerns as an explorative poet.

Larkin is a complex social poet because of the doubleness of his vision, because of the tension which exists between his poetry of criticism and his poetry of praise. And his capacity for praise should be seen for the imaginative goodwill and such moral courage as it contains. At its most eloquent, that praise moves deliberately toward those fleeting sensations of harmony which also characterise his poetry of solitary wonder at the elements. Larkin does not give us a social ideology. What we are given instead are analysis and a sense of mystery as they compete with one another throughout the poet's chronicle. 'In other words,' Larkin has remarked, 'good social and political literature can exist only if it originates in the imagination, and it will do that only if the imagination finds the subject exciting, and not because the intellect thinks it important; and it will succeed only in so far as the imagination's original concept has been realized.'[7] What Larkin's imagination finds 'exciting' when he takes an open stance next to his society is the small beauty of festive community events, commonplace life as it shares in ritual beauty. His contribution to the social literature of the post-war period lies in his ability to notice, and record, that there is a beauty in the commonplace which persists, and also a delicate and spontaneous unity which can sometimes preside.

Larkin's social vision is analogous to his existential vision in

that he writes out on both levels his thinking and feeling response
to the bleakness he perceives while at the same time remaining
alert to the traces of beauty which can be salvaged from the plane
of the elemental world and the living reality of ordinary life. Daily
life and the natural world yield up arresting insights to the poet
and he records them and moves on to the next experience. Because
he writes from sensations as they arise, it is not easy fully to
measure the weight of his moments of exceptional connection with
either the natural or the human worlds; it is difficult, that is, to do
so without erasing the essential dynamic of the poet's explorative
art. Very like Lawrence, Larkin refuses to state the fullest
meaning of these moments of illumination in the abstract. Yet it is
certain that for both artists the value of the experiences is strong.
They are connected to a will toward spiritual health and they exist
as moments of hope which diminish a strong tendency toward
pessimism.

There is a religious dimension to the kinds of experience we
witness in such poems as 'The Whitsun Weddings', 'To the Sea'
and 'Show Saturday', just as this is also the case in Larkin's poems
of wonder at the elements. And, when Lawrence tried to state the
full power of such moments of connection, he said that they are
exceptional in that they give us a 'feeling' for 'that which exists in
non-dimensional space', a feeling for what is 'deathless, lifeless,
and eternal'.[8] Larkin similarly holds that the most successful of
his poems 'float free from the preoccupations that chose them' and
are 'reassembled – one hopes – in the eternity of the imagination'.[9]
This is about as close as one can come, I think, to asserting the
possibility of a transcendent world without naming it. And yet it is
in the very nature of Lawrence's and Larkin's sense of mystery
that they must keep their diction on the matter designedly vague.
Their wonder is of a kind which remains close to the earth and
issues forth from the plane of observation as something profound
but elusive. It is seen, appreciated and re-created in art; so it is
there on the page as substantial and as involved in the immediacy
of the writer's words and his world at once. As such, it is the index
of a way of consciousness rather than a philosophical or religious
metaphysic. Both Lawrence and Larkin are undeniably major
artists in their nourishment of this passing wonder in their art.

Poetry is about the bearing of the mind next to reality, and it is
arguable that the modern imagination is a dislocated one in that
the 'immediacy' central to Lawrence's purchase on the world is so

rare that we value it as a primer to recovering a connection with the surrounding human and natural universe.[10] So there is a very powerful way in which the kind of art we experience in the works of Lawrence and Larkin can be said to have a value separate or surplus to the local thematic concerns which are there in the details of individual works. As artists who are exceptionally alert to the literal plane of reality, Lawrence and Larkin encourage in their audience a curiosity next to reality which is rewarded by experiences of such unusual awareness that we are forced to name these moments ones of epiphany. In the depth of their meaning, the moments lift the mind out of the ordinary and point to what Lawrence termed 'non-dimensional space' and to what Larkin names 'the eternity of the imagination'. Their art, that is to say, is ultimately an art of consciousness in all of its imaginative alertness, of the mind in astute bearing next to the world; it is an art of immediacy.

Larkin and Lawrence are poets of both theme and epiphany. As thematic poets they write in the tradition of English poetry which existed before the complicated narrative revolution of the early part of this century. Yet as poets of epiphany and beholding observation they participate in the twentieth-century inclination toward a poetry of concreteness and attentiveness to the details of the empirical world. It is undeniable that the Imagist aspect of the Modernist revolution in the arts, therefore, has a relationship – however modified – to their concerns as artists of reality. As Colin Falck has put it, it was the Imagists who 'cranked the engine of twentieth-century poetry even if it was left to others to take the car on its journey', and 'Another look at what Imagism did and did not do for poetry might renew some poetic hopes on both sides of the Atlantic at the present time.'[11] And even though, as William Pratt accurately states it, 'Imagist poetry itself is a minor poetry',[12] the imprint of the Imagists' desire to reconnect the mind with the minutiae of outward reality is there in the work of such major writers as Lawrence and Larkin, as it is also vigorously present in the work of Larkin's proper contemporary peers. As poets of both epiphany and theme, Lawrence and Larkin show that the astute observing graces of the early Imagist poets can be transformed into a wider dimension of expression which is more intent, personal and narratively sophisticated than the kind of poetry we witness in, for instance, Pratt's collection *The Imagist Poem* (1963). What the work of Larkin, especially, shows is that the Imagist bearing of mind next to reality can be modified into a kind of poetry more humanised and richer in the range of its thematic concerns. Larkin is a traditional poet in his adherence to traditional form and in his writing of a poetry of discourse and personal expression; but as a poet of epiphany he participates in the most durable tradition of twentieth-century poetry, the Imagist vein of Modernism.

Even amidst Larkin's concerns as an unillusioned neo-Augustan poet we have seen the value of T. E. Hulme's aesthetic in its suggestions about the limits of traditional Romanticism. And in the minutiae of Larkin's craft as a poet observing epiphany it becomes obvious that it is because he indeed does absorb the finest wisdom of the Modernist revolution that he can be lauded as a late Imagist poet. In addition, the ultimate convenience for the critic, in these matters, lies in the fact that it is precisely because of the *kind* of poetry he writes, as a late Imagist, that all issues about the finality of his vision melt away when considered next to his aesthetic of poetry, an aesthetic which is open, explorative and epiphanic.

6 Poetry of Reality

Larkin is a poet of reality in the sense that the real world is never very far away in his work, and it is commonly at the centre of his thematic concerns. In his reviews and commentaries he continually underlines the value of what we have heard Lawrence name the 'wholeness of man wholly attending'. There is a disposition of mind which is central to Larkin's personae – regardless of their different emotional biases – and it is an empirical, attending one. In a very broad manner he connects his art with the example of Lawrence, Hardy, the Romantics, and the middle perspective on reality of much poetry of the English past by virtue of this wholeness of observation. His poetry can be said to be traditional in its maintenance of this vigorous capacity for alertness to the familiar world.

Moreover, there is a way in which that 'wholeness' of attending was turned inward by the Symbolist dimension of the Modernist revolution in that, whereas concreteness of symbol and metaphor is present in, for instance, the practice of T. S. Eliot, it is a concreteness which serves the potentially obscure symbology that is involved in the poem. Reality is present in the typical Modernist masterpiece, but it is transformed into an objective correlative for a rarefied statement about the poet's spiritual quest. In short, and simplifying quite deliberately, there is a way in which the Modernist purchase on reality, at its most Symbolistic height, mines reality for symbol rather than bodying forth reality as a living presence. The world of the Modernist poem is not the familiar world; it is a landscape of the mind in which concrete metaphors, images and symbols act as the signifiers of a complex state of spiritual internality. Much of its brilliance is contained in this removed kind of effect, but Larkin has demonstrated that he is impatient with the inevitable obscurity of such poetry, and his comments in this regard have distracted his readers from a different and specifically Imagist aesthetic which is at the core of his own poetic practice.

Evaluating the technical cleverness of Modernist jazz musicians, Larkin has written that, 'I dislike such things not because they are new, but because they are irresponsible exploitations of technique in contradiction of life as we know it. This is my essential criticism of modernism, whether perpetuated by Parker, or Pound or Picasso: it helps us neither to enjoy nor endure.'[1] Modernist art is given to obscurity without profundity, is inclined to pretentiousness because it takes us away from 'life as we know it'. In an interview with Ian Hamilton, he has also expressed his reservations this way:

> What I do feel a bit rebellious about is that poetry seems to have got into the hands of a critical industry which is concerned with culture in the abstract, and this I do rather lay at the door of Eliot and Pound. . . . I think a lot of the 'myth-kitty' business has grown out of that, because first of all you have to be terribly educated, you have to read everything to know these things, and secondly you've got somehow to work them in. But to me . . . the whole of classical and biblical mythology means very little, and I think that using them today not only fills poems full of dead spots but dodges the writer's duty to be original.[2]

Given such reservations, it is no surprise that his critics have until recently been in the habit of discussing his poetry away from the Modernists and next to the work of such figures as the Georgians, or discussing it in the context of the more immediate tradition of the Movement poets, when thinking of the poetry of the twentieth century.[3]

Yet it is primarily the bookish–allusive obscurity of the Modernists which annoys Larkin's critical temperament, and even amidst a more recent restatement of his dislike of this escape from the familiar world ('It seems to me undeniable that up to this century literature used language in the way we all use it, painting represented what anyone with normal vision sees . . .'[4]) he shows that the preoccupation with the real perception we associate with the Imagists at least hints that his rejection of Modernism is specialised, and in argument only with its more cryptic dimensions, those which involve an attenuation of reality.

Larkin is a poet of sympathetic observation, undoubtedly, and his own literary criticism is punctuated with comments which have an Imagist ring to them. His rejection of allusive obscurity in the practice of such poets as T. S. Eliot and Ezra Pound is no more than a healthy cynicism about their more pedantic and elitist gestures, and his own poetry is in rhythm with a widely Imagist kind of purchase on the world. Robert Conquest was to say that Movement poetry is 'empirical in its attitude to all that comes',[5] a statement which provokes one to notice that Larkin is essentially a poet of sensation and impression, a craftsman who enacts something like the wisdom of Wallace Stevens's claim that 'The greatest poverty is not to live / In the physical world'.[6] Larkin is exceptionally alert to the surface suggestions of the immediate physical world, and he is also a poet of epiphany. In this basically Imagist bias of his art we can see the majority of his finest visual effects. And in the anti-romantic nature of at least T. E. Hulme's Imagist theory, we have already seen at work the consonance of his art with an Imagist poetry of passing wonder and restraint.

Most of Larkin's poetry is engaged in visual participation in the observable physical world. His speakers often beckon the reader, as they do in Hardy's poetry, into a beholding-process. 'Look', says the speaker in 'Home is so Sad', at 'the pictures and the cutlery / The music in the piano stool. That vase' (*WW*, p. 17). This kind of invitation to witness is not simply an accident of form; it is the result of an epistemological conviction that the truth – as Larkin sees it – is inseparable from an attending alertness of mind ('When I see a couple of kids', begins the speaker in 'High Windows' – *HW*, p. 17). In a central way, Larkin's speakers are like the passengers on the train in 'The Whitsun Weddings'; they are 'loaded with the sum of all they saw' (*WW*, p. 22). What we, as readers, see is the product of the engagement of an empirical intelligence and a flexible poetic personality with the face of reality. We are involved in the process by proxy, join the perceptual journey in so far as we are willing to respond to the substance and suggestiveness of the world as he presents it. The reader does not venture far in Larkin's world unless he participates in the speaker's curious glance. Any concentrated experience of Larkin's poetry includes the visual process of looking, noticing, gazing, even staring, at the world, as it is carefully re-created in its ordinary and then extraordinary detail. The most casual sorting of his lines in this regard gives evidence of at least *his* insistence on the importance of the process:

Look down at the yard. Outside seems old enough:

Red brick, lagged pipes, and someone walking by it
Out to the car park, free.

('The Building', *HW*, p. 25)

One sees, with a sharp tender shock,
His hand withdrawn, holding her hand.

('An Arundel Tomb', *WW*, p. 45)

My swivel eye hungers from pose to pose. . . .
('Lines on a Young Lady's Photograph Album', *LD*, p. 13)

The eye can hardly pick them out
From the cold shade they shelter in,
Till the wind distresses tail and mane. . . .

('At Grass', *LD*, p. 45)

The eye sees you
Simplified by distance
Into an origin. . . .

('Solar', *HW*, p. 33)

Latest face, so effortless
Your great arrival at my eyes. . . .

('Latest Face', *LD*, p. 41)

One shivers slightly, looking up there.

('Sad Steps', *HW*, p. 32)

In what amounts to a habit of beholding visual sensitivity, he
aligns his art with the tradition of empirically oriented poetry
which reaches back through most of the great poetry of the
English language tradition. The centre of gravity in Larkin's
poetry is the physical world as it suggestively manifests itself on
the stage of his personal imagination. The examples of Lawrence,
of Hardy especially, and of the Imagist theorists of the early part

of this century have played a large part in this beholding-emphasis in his work. The Imagists attempted to retrieve the empirical health of poetry for this century, and their effect carries through poets such as Wallace Stevens and William Carlos Williams on through to the richest poetry of the post-war period.

There is a kinship between Larkin's critical attention to empirical writing and the similarly pictorial bias of the Imagist theorists. In a recent comment on 'the poet' he stressed the need for the poet to 'recreate the familiar'.[7] He commends William Barnes because his 'view of nature is clear . . . and shining, full of exquisite pictorial miniatures'.[8] Conversely, in his review of Auden's *Homage to Clio* (1960), Larkin regrets the intrusion of a new 'abstract windiness' into Auden's style, censoriously noting Auden's need to find 'root again in the life surrounding him rather than in his reading'.[9] He praises Betjeman because in him 'the eye leads the spirit',[10] and we can add to this his claim that Betjeman holds a belief 'that a poem's meaning should be communicated directly and not by symbol',[11] and his notice of Betjeman's 'astonishing command of detail, both visual and circumstantial'.[12] Furthermore, when he pays tribute to Hardy's ability 'often [to] be extremely direct'[13] in his treatment of the real world, and recognises Hardy's talent for 'a kind of telescoping of a couple of images',[14] he points to qualities which remind us that Hardy is a major figure in the maintenance of the imagistic base of English poetry.[15] On such evidence we recognise in Larkin's concerns, and immediately in his phrasing of them, a connection with the language of Hulme and Pound. Phrases such as 'extremely direct', 'exquisite pictorial natures' and 'telescoping of a couple of images' are continuous with – if not direct echoes of – the terminology of the Imagist theorists and their creative imitators throughout the twentieth century.

If we go briefly back to the early Imagist theorists, we recall their desire to animate again the empirical basis of thought and art, and in that aim we can recognise many of Larkin's own concerns. Thus, in a language which is akin to Larkin's own critical standards, there is Hulme's comment that 'Poetry . . . is not a counter language, but a visual concrete one. It is a compromise for a language of intuition which would hand over sensations bodily. It always endeavours to arrest you, and to make you continuously see a physical thing, to prevent you gliding through an abstract process.'[16] For Hulme, this is not a matter of merely contriving a concrete metaphor in the work, but rather has to do with the empirical authenticity of the thought process which the poem embodies. The poem is conceived as a re-creation of the physical world as perceived in a moment of unusually alert attention to the meaning of its face. This leads Hulme to say, 'Whenever you get an extraordinary interest in a thing, a great zest in its contemplation . . . you have justification for poetry.' For him the critical litmus test of a poem, what makes it 'authentic', is its 'freshness', a freshness which is difficult to sham: 'Freshness convinces you, you feel at once that the artist was in an actual physical state. You feel that for a minute.'[17] It is a comment which is in step with Pound's directive that the poet must 'use his *image* because he sees or feels it, *not* because he thinks he can use it to back up some system of ethics or economics'[18] – a comment which sounds like an early version of Larkin's scorn for 'myth-kitty' and for poetry as ideology.

Much of Larkin's poetry centrally and exclusively contains a good deal of that 'zest' and that 'freshness' of which Hulme speaks. It is there, for instance, in the virtual tumble of detail from the physical world which is at the living base of his poem of praise 'Show Saturday'. It is a poem which has a crowded life of its own, a Brueghel-like grasp of the immediacy of life's plural detail:

> In the main arena, more judges meet by a jeep:
> The jumping's on next. Announcement, splutteringly loud,
>
> Clash with the quack of a man with pound notes round his hat
> And a lit-up board. There's more than just animals:
> Bread-stalls, balloon-men, a Bank; a beer-marquee that
> Half-screens a canvass Gents; a tent selling tweed,
> And another, jackets. Folks sit about on bales
> Like great straw dice. For each scene is linked by spaces
> Not given to anything much, where kids scrap, freed,
> While their owners stare different ways with incurious faces.
>
> The wrestling starts, late; a wide ring of people; then cars;
> Then trees; then pale sky. Two young men in acrobats' tights
> And embroidered trunks hug each other; rock over the grass,
> Stiff-legged, in a two-man scrum. One falls: they shake hands.

Two more start, one gray-haired: he wins, though. They're not
   so much fights
As long immobile strainings that end in unbalance
With one on his back, unharmed, while the other stands
Smoothing his hair. But there are other talents. . . .

(*HW*, p. 37)

The 'zest' continues in a celebratory rendering of a freshly animated imagery of objects, people and their gestures. In its observation of the plural tumble of life it is reminiscent of Louis MacNeice and also of what Randall Jarrell has termed the 'empirical gaiety'[19] of poets such as William Carlos Williams – another poet who extracted an imagist bias from the Modernists without participating in that tradition's more cryptic conventions. This is an effect which we have seen Larkin also manage within his Lawrentian focus in 'The Whitsun Weddings' and 'To the Sea'. It is attributable to his conscious maintenance of the English tradition and to his kinship with Hardy and the Imagists' view of the poem as the act of the mind dealing with its sensations and impressions of the immediate world.

But it is the conviction neither of the Imagist theorists nor of Larkin that poetry is only the act of the imagination in continual representation of the world's plenitude. The mistake of many of the early Imagist poets (as opposed to its best theorists) was that they mistook simple selection of objects for saying something profound. The quality of freshness is there as part of Larkin's authenticating reality, but the expressive dimension of his poetry transforms the attending glance into something much larger, more interesting and coherent; we have seen Larkin do this in poems influenced by the example of Johnson, Hardy and Lawrence. For Larkin, the poet also has a personality and an explorative vision to express. An impression of the world is at the stimulating base of the work, but there is also a process of thought regarding the impression which he conveys. In this sense, he can be said to take the Imagist theorists more seriously than did many of the early Imagist practitioners.

Larkin's imagist impulse is visible in the process of empirical thought which is embodied in each of his poems separately. Each poem evokes the world and ponders it without leaving it behind. It is for this reason that his symbolic effects are natural, and seem to rise inevitably from within the context of the poem's individual setting. Such a strategy of form is at work in the exploratory observations of 'Church Going', 'The Old Fools' and 'High Windows', for example. The symbolism which these representative poems embody is that which Pound describes as

> *Symbols.* – I believe that the proper and perfect symbol is the natural object, that if man uses 'symbols' he must so use them that their symbolic function does not obtrude; so that a sense, and the poetic quality of the passage, is not lost to those who do not understand the symbol as such, to whom, for instance, a hawk is a hawk.[20]

Larkin is a contemporary master of exactly this kind of an effect, and it is one which he admires greatly in the work of Hardy, Lawrence and Betjeman. The physical bearing of the church in 'Church Going', for instance, is rendered as evidence of the poet's thematic point about the decline of traditional belief. A survey of its details shows it to be a living index of all the values it once more certainly embodied. And, in Larkin's evocation of the physical fact of the hospital in 'The Building', the empirical intelligence of the poet registers it as a naturally symbolic expression of the human desire to build this structure physically and spiritually into a substitute cathedral:

> Higher than the handsomest hotel
> The lucent comb shows up for miles, but see,
> All round it close-ribbed streets rise and fall
> Like a great sigh out of the last century.
> The porters are scruffy; what keep drawing up
> At the entrance are not taxis; and in the hall
> As well as creepers hangs a frightening smell.

> (*HW*, p. 24)

The circumstantial contemplation of the poem proceeds from here through another ten stanzas. As the speaker wanders through the hospital's sights, he gathers images of the fearful faces of the entering patients. The gestures of the patients accumulate into a compelling imaginative logic, one in which the stock natural symbolism of the hospital as a substitute church is finally questioned. On the basis of the speaker's witness of the setting, he deduces that the proper metaphor for the hospital is that of a prison. 'O world', he says in the sixth stanza, 'Your loves, your chances, are beyond the stretch / Of any hand from here!' (*HW*, p. 25). And, as the cumulative impression of the hospital reaches a cohering moment of integrity, he expresses the meaning of the building in a manner of saddened empirical discovery. The hospital is a natural symbol, not of healing, but of the undeniable fact of death. In keeping with its consistent use of natural symbolism, the gloomy figure concludes his experiential journey through the physical visage of the place by saying of the patients that

> All know they are going to die.
> Not yet, perhaps not here, but in the end,
> And somewhere like this. This is what it means,
> This clean-sliced cliff; a struggle to transcend
> The thought of dying, for unless its powers
> Outbuild cathedrals nothing contravenes
> The coming dark, though crowds each evening try
>
> With wasteful, weak, propitiatory flowers.

> (*HW*, pp. 25–6)

'The Building' deals thematically with the inadequacy of modern man's attempt to outbuild death with a new faith in medicine and technology. Ironically, the very attempt to defeat death is seen as an evasion of its presence. All of the appearance of control is an illusion and yet the fix we are in is that religious illusions are seen as even less adequate. Up the street from the hospital is a 'locked church'. The natural symbolism of that fact is compelling evidence for the speaker's case. Hence, in a contemplation in which the physical world is intimately involved in the process of thought, the speaker accumulates his observation into a dismally accurate conclusion, given the circumstances. To use a phrase from 'Lines on a Young Lady's Photograph Album', what is 'In every sense empirically true' (*LD*, p. 13) about the hospital is its visible testimony of our pathetic weakness in the face of the mortality which it tries to outbuild. The 'wasteful, weak, propitiatory flowers' complete the foray into reality, and they are moved sadly out of the stanzaic pattern as a way of housing them as an imagist epiphany, the discovery of a telling clue. The flowers, in their naturally symbolic effect, are analogous to the fragility of the human being, its frail beauty. They project a bitterly ironic truth: for all of their smallness, there is more meaning in their failure (and in the compassion they also reflect) than in the illusion of longevity which the 'clean-sliced cliff' of the building unsuccessfully projects.

It was Stevens who said, echoing the Imagists, that 'Much of the world of fact is the equivalent of the world of imagination',[21] which is a conviction at the centre of Larkin's achievement. Further, the world of fact is uninteresting or downright mute unless it is sifted and rearranged into meaning by the unifying intelligence of the poet, and by, in the case of Larkin, his simultaneously ironic and wondrous sensibility. The poet's colouring of the facts of the world by his poetic personality and his thematic compulsions takes all major poetry of immediacy far past a mere suspension of objects. Neither Larkin nor Stevens claims that the poem of reality is an objectively verifiable medium of truth. Stevens has said that 'Poetry is an unofficial view of being',[22] and Larkin, I think, would agree. But it is worth recognising that the poetry of this order does mimic the inductive method and can be said to be more directly experiential than more confidently mythic poetry. On the basis of that distinction it is given therefore to an openness to experience, and an intelligence of the senses which more traditional mythic poetry often tends to lack. Grounded in actual observation, each poem becomes – as Larkin once described it – its 'own sole freshly-created universe', and has an integrity in the recognisable world of experience.

The subjective dimension of the poem lies in the fact that it is precisely the personality of the poet which enables him to realise a meaning in what he sees. It is the emotional colouring of the personae which gives a uniqueness to the particular visions embodied in the physical world of the given poem. Thus, it is the familiar ironic persona of Larkin's 'Mr Bleaney', for example, which colours the world which that poem embodies. The world perceived in the poem is one which that particular persona has an inclination to recognise. Paradoxically, the persona's limitation of perception is his very qualification for the uniqueness of his moment of vision.

Larkin finds the reality of the sub-heroic Mr Bleaney indexed in the physical facts of Bleaney's room. The prosaic quality of Bleaney's existence is captured in the beholding observation of the poet. His eye collects impressions in a journey toward comprehension:

> Flowered curtains, thin and frayed,
> Fall to within five inches of the sill,
>
> Whose window shows a strip of building land,
> Tussocky, littered. 'Mr Bleaney took
> My bit of garden properly in hand.'
> Bed, upright chair, sixty-watt bulb, no hook
>
> Behind the door, no room for books or bags –
> 'I'll take it.' So it happens that I lie
> Where Mr Bleaney lay, and stub my fags
> On the same saucer-souvenir. . . .

> (*WW*, p. 10)

The objects selected to comprise the contemplation have all the freshness and realistic presence which Hulme stated as necessary to the image. But the ordering of the images, the connecting of the spaces between them, is the cohering-process which gives the poem its true brilliance. There is a unifying quality in all of the central images, an essence which is noticed and abstracted. At the same time the process of thought is stated in the natural symbolism of the objects, just as they are also collected into a perceptible whole. We observe the dearth of aesthetic demeanour in Bleaney's room, and how the 'Tussocky, littered' strip of building-land shares with the equally tussocky curtains, light bulb and minimally functional furniture an unkempt, unfinished quality which signifies Bleaney's life. Significantly, it is because the speaker detects a similarly tossed clumsiness in the sky that he can consent to a respect for Bleaney's unambitious and awkwardly low-keyed existence:

> But if he stood and watched the frigid wind
> Tousling the clouds, lay on the fusty bed
> Telling himself that this was home, and grinned,
> And shivered, without shaking off the dread

> That how we live measures our own nature,
> And at his age having no more to show
> Than one hired box should make him pretty sure
> He warranted no better, I don't know.

(WW, p. 10)

The 'frigid wind / Tousling the clouds' bears an analogous relation to the 'strip of land / Tussocky, littered'. The sounds of the phrases are even analogous to the similar look of the pictures. Because of this ragged quality which is noticed in all selected details of the scene, Bleaney's life is perceived as having a kind of sanction for its prosiness which is realised as somehow written into the scheme of things. There are people like Bleaney, implies the speaker, just as there are days and settings like the one here evoked. Bleaney represents a great deal of reality. In the poet's foray into that reality in this particular 'sole freshly-created universe', there is an attending recognition of this truth. And, in terms of Imagist theory, the poem passes the test: there is an illusion that, in Hulme's words, 'the artist was in an actual physical state', and, in the participating-experience of reading the poem, 'You feel that for a minute.'

Of course, in the poetic process the poet also expresses a view of reality. The real is the stimulus and is also an integral part of the thinking-process of the poem. And the poet's personality plays a central part in the colouring of the real, just as the real often challenges the colour of his view, altering its shade and sometimes changing his view quite radically. The imagist focus in Larkin's work is always part of a larger interest in personal expression, usually of new personal discovery in the complex conversation with bleakness and beauty that takes place between the poet and his world. Characteristically, the speaker in 'Mr Bleaney' says finally, 'I don't know', a qualifying gesture which states that the epiphany of existential raggedness in the poem is not embraced as a controlling and final statement of his own complete view. Larkin's placing self-scepticism is at work here, a self-doubt that amounts to the openness which will free him to respond to other aspects of reality in other poems, next to other realities.

In 'Mr Bleaney' the persona Larkin adopts is the one which he finds most appropriate to the setting which he confronts. But his settings, like his personae, are not especially chosen to be dreary ones, just as the epiphany which rises from the setting does not always match the appearance of the setting as we are first led to view it. If, for instance, we turn to 'Dublinesque', the 'freshly-created universe' is, as the poet's poetic demands, *'freshly . . . created'*. The speaker in 'Dublinesque' wears the familiar persona of poignant sadness, and also embodies Larkin's undervalued capacity for praise. In its registration of a complicated moment of epiphany, it accords in spirit with the subtlety of the Imagists' view in this regard. Its careful achievement characterises the Imagist requirement that the poem represents a moment of suggestive illumination out of the context of the immediate world:

> Down stucco sidestreets,
> Where light is pewter
> And afternoon mist
> Brings lights on in shops
> Above race-guides and rosaries,
> A funeral passes.
>
> The hearse is ahead,
> But after there follows
> A troop of streetwalkers
> In wide flowered hats,
> Leg-of-mutton sleeves,
> And ankle-length dresses.
>
> There is an air of great friendliness,
> As if they were honouring
> One they were fond of;
> Some caper a few steps,
> Skirts held skilfully
> (Someone claps time),
>
> And of a great sadness also.
> As they wend away
> A voice is heard singing
> Of Kitty, or Katy,
> As if the name meant once
> All love, all beauty.

(*HW*, p. 28)

'Poetry increases the feeling for reality',[23] says Stevens in a comment appropriate to this poem. And in 'Dublinesque' the feeling takes the shape of an intimate contact with an entire culture. There is an imagist pictorial visibility to the scene, and the speaker's empirical imagination searches out and focuses the living reality of its physical world. The juxtaposition of the 'race-guides and rosaries' telescopes two contradictory images between which blossoms a shrewd comment about the life and culture of Dublin. Larkin is here in effortless company with Joyce, giving us an immediate sense of the culture, its physical–spiritual reality. 'Dublinesque' embodies a moment of epiphany, one in which the ostensible contradictions in the visible scene are blended musically into an illumination of beauty. The illumination is based on a perception of a quality which pervades life in Dublin like the 'afternoon mist' which so evanescently suggests its surface. Hence, while the fact of the funeral initially appears in odd contradiction to the gaiety of the funeral party – a gaiety caught in the speaker's participation in the life of the middle stanzas – the attending consciousness accumulates the particulars of the scene into something more profound. At its centre is the recognition of a poignantly beautiful quality in the life which is witnessed. As in 'Home is so Sad', there is a recognition of a spirited courage in the energy of the people, one which saves the speaker from a simply pathetic conclusion, a conclusion which his sad persona might be prone to veer toward. The sound of the voice 'singing / Of Kitty, or Katy' rises from the scene of daily life as audibly appropriate to the imagery. In that sound, and in the sight of the face of reality in the poem, it rises as a very Irish version of a Wordsworthian 'still, sad music of humanity', one which is compassionate and also energetic. Larkin's respect for it shows in an ascending tone of praise and celebration which turns the epiphany about prosaic ritual into song.

The close interplay, the conversation, between spirit and the physical world is the fulcrum on which the poise of Larkin's poetry and also his poetic rest. His personae, each of whom is governed by an attending intelligence, show a willingness to move exploratively into the living detail of actually observed or imagined physical worlds. Larkin himself sees the act of re-creating the experience from which the poem takes its inception to be an act of victory over time, and his statement on the matter echoes the Imagist conviction that the work of art is the expression of life's rarest moments of realisation, the poet's moments of epiphany. It is a conviction which he shares with Lawrence, and is also in great measure expressed in his aesthetic in an Imagist critical diction. With the experience of 'Dublinesque' present as example, one recognises, for example, the definite and detailed Imagist ring to the following comment by Larkin:

> I write poems to preserve things I have seen/thought/felt (if I may so indicate a composite and complex experience) both for myself and for others, though I feel that my prime responsibility is to the experience itself, which I am trying to keep from oblivion for its own sake. Why I should do this I have no idea, but I think the impulse to preserve lies at the bottom of all art.[24]

Larkin significantly emphasises a close connection between seeing, thinking and feeling. In his view, each poem re-creates a real perception and moves it upward to transcend time in the qualified way the work of art can. In his statement of his preserving instinct he echoes Lawrence, and also the Imagist notion once expressed by Hulme, that 'Literature, like memory, selects only the vivid patches of life', and that in a sense 'Life is composed of exquisite moments and the rest is only shadows of them.'[25] Larkin's comment on his motivation to preserve not only frames the achievement of 'Dublinesque', but also brings to mind Pound's famous description of the 'Image' and his description of its epiphanic effect of managing a victory over time and place. When the writer successfully conveys the complexity of the experience which Larkin has termed a 'seen/thought/felt' one, he approximates the 'Image' Pound similarly described as

> that which represents an intellectual and emotional complex in an instant of time. . . . It is the presentation of such a 'complex' instantaneously which gives the sense of a sudden liberation; that sense of freedom from time limits and space limits; that sense of sudden growth, which we experience in the presence of the greatest works of art.[26]

Both Pound and Larkin, in directly comparable terminology, express a view of art centrally concerned with the registration of a moment of perception in time that seems to transcend our more ordinary awareness of life. Of course, it is a classic definition of the artist that the artist is the one who sees/thinks/feels more than other people and is able to articulate the complexity of the attendant insights. The artist is the person who makes public a diary of perceptive moments. 'Dublinesque' and the vast majority of Larkin's poems carefully enact the process involved in the selection of the 'vivid patches of life' which he has deemed worth transforming into public statement. 'Dublinesque' is an act of preservation of a thing which is 'seen/thought/felt'. In the empirical sharpness of its imagist base, and in the characteristic sensitivity of its triumph, it is the registration of a moment of the poet's felt connection with his momentarily coherent world.

Looking back over the critical record, we realise that it is Anthony Thwaite who tells us the most in the least number of words about Larkin when he writes that 'What Hardy taught Larkin was that a man's own life, its suddenly surfacing perceptions, its "moments of vision", its most seemingly casual epiphanies (in the Joycean sense), could fit whole and without compromise into poems'.[27] Moments of epiphany are of central importance in Larkin's work, and it is the example not only of Hardy but also of Lawrence and the Imagists, and of a series of minor poets such as Barnes and Betjeman, which encourages him in continually returning to the plane of living and primarily ordinary reality for the passing truths which make up his chronicle of epiphanies. The complexity and delicacy of his art lies precisely in the scrupulously re-created difficulty of perception these moments embody. At the height of his powers he transcends the ordinary limits of awareness and moves to that 'lift off the ground'[28] (to borrow his own locution for the final effect intended in 'The Whitsun Weddings') commonly associated with the poetry of vision.

Other critics have found it convenient to discuss Larkin's accomplishment as one which verges on a Symbolist wisdom, and there is of course a way in which particular cases of Symbolist and Imagist practice are in close proximity in their desire to lift the objects of this world into an indefinite suggestion of a more permanent one. But I have controlled my temptation to proceed further along this interesting avenue primarily because it threatens to distract attention from the way Larkin grounds his art in living and ordinary reality to a degree which keeps him close to Hulme and Lawrence's 'passing wonder' – and at the same time leaves the plane of the real intact. Symbolist poetry is given to disfiguring reality to an extent which Larkin, in both his poetry and his aesthetic, has tried for the most part to avoid. And finally to name Larkin a dominantly 'Symbolist' poet is also, I think, to run the risk of placing too much emphasis on his concerns with another world beyond this one. Larkin, at his most intensely religious and 'almost' atoned, is a poet of passing wonder at best. Nor does he share with many Symbolist practitioners a subjectivism and removal from the world of living experience which so often moves poetry into that realm of obscurity which he so abjures in Modernist practice.

The extent to which Larkin is a transcendent poet is both limited and liberating. He is an intuitive poet who refuses to turn his intuitions into myth or ideology, leaving the reader with a chronicle rather than a system of epiphanies. Again, it is in Hulme that Larkin's proximity to Imagist theory and to Symbolist preoccupation with transcendence is given its best definition. Further to his definition of the 'classical in verse', which serves to express the cautious quality of modern wonder, there are Hulme's words on the relationship between intuitive synthesis and the hunger of the ordinary intellect for system. Describing the depth and also the elusive quality of epiphanic poetry he writes,

> The intellect always analyses – when there is a synthesis it is baffled. That is why the artist's work seems mysterious. The intellect can't represent it. This is a necessary consequence of the particular nature of the intellect and the purposes for which it is formed. It doesn't mean that your synthesis is ineffable, simply that it can't be definitely stated.
>
> Now this is all worked out in Bergson, the central feature of his whole philosophy. It is all based on the clear conception of these vital complexities which he calls 'intensive' as opposed to the other kind which he calls 'extensive', and the recognition of the fact that the intellect can only deal with extensive multiplicity. To deal with the intensive you must use intuition.[29]

Wallace Stevens restates this intractable identity with intuitive art when he reminds us that poetry at its height is a 'pheasant disappearing in the brush',[30] and embodies a 'miracle of logic' in its intensive rather than extensive approach to the truth:

The truth seems to be that we live in concepts of the imagination before the reason has established them. If this is true, then reason is simply the methodizer of the imagination. It may be that the imagination is a miracle of logic and that its exquisite divinations are calculations beyond analysis, as the conclusions of the reason are calculations wholly within analysis. . . . Of what value is anything to the solitary and those that live in misery and terror, except the imagination?[31]

Larkin is a poet of reality who, as result of his explorations, turns up his 'intensive' moments, his epiphanies, as individual 'miracle[s] of logic', and he refused to methodise his imagination in spite of his critics' impatience with his unwillingness to do so. The upshot is that criticism has tended intolerantly to abstract a view of reality from any given poem, or single cluster of poems, and to forge a conclusiveness to the poet's vision and name it the poet's own.

But the first and last responsibility of the critic, given the *kind* of poetry that Larkin writes, is, I think, to recognise the various facets of the poet's personality, his themes, interests, and – especially in Larkin's case – the explorative nature of his vision. Larkin is neither a defeated nor a reconciled poet; and that statement holds true for his personal, social and existential dimensions as a writer all at once. As a poet of reality he turns up both epiphanies of void and epiphanies of passing wonder, and it is not possible (though the critical intellect might wish otherwise) to add up his competing insights in a way that brings about a strictly measurable final statement. Looking back over the chronicle of his epiphanies, there seems no reason to assume that he found adequate reasons for resolving the dialectic of his poetry into a purely pessimistic or simply atoned vision.

Quite recently, when invited to name what he thought were his most typical poems, Larkin replied, 'I don't think any of my poems are more typical of me than the rest. "The Whitsun Weddings", "The Explosion", "Show Saturday", "Coming", "Absences" – no, I can't pick and choose. "Send No Money" is the one I repeat to myself. Don't judge me by them. Some are better than me, but I add up to more than they do.'[32] The most interesting aspect of these comments is their implication that the poet, at this juncture, prefers his poems about the residual beauty in life to those consonant with his reputation as a poet of the 'true'.

If nothing else, his musings on his choices stand as proof that his 'miseries are overdone a bit by the critics'.[33] At this stage it is safe to conclude that, while Larkin's poetry was first brought to our attention as the poetry of an unillusioned man, it should last into the future as the work of an artist who has taken a creative attitude to his gloom and explored living reality for such instances or traces of beauty as survive the wasteland aspect of the twentieth century.

In the end, Larkin is memorable, a major poet, for more than the range of his personality and thematic interests. The kind of art that he has mastered, an art of immediacy and openness to meaning, constitutes one of the most satisfying signs of the survival of the human spirit past the fatigue and boredom of modern subjectivism. It is obvious that I have credited the Imagists, Hardy and Lawrence for what amounts to a recovery of curiosity about the world in Larkin's volumes, but the creative transformation of their influences in his work is also distinctive in its rigorous application of such past wisdom to the spiritual issues of contemporary life. It has long been my conviction that the Imagist and the Lawrentian legacy to twentieth-century literature has been underestimated, and the rich influence on Larkin in this regard is one of the most vital points of reference we have for evidence of this oversight.

Significantly, the Imagist and Lawrentian influence on the poetry of today brings with it the possibility of a spiritual health of an order that is almost inconceivable in many of the subjective Modernist masterpieces of the early part of the century, or in much so-called 'confessional' contemporary writing. The hunger for further meaning, an openness to beauty and the value of the small human being, and a profound curiosity about life outside the confines of books are all visible in the Lawrentian and Imagist influence on Larkin and, I shall shortly claim, visible in this influence on those who I would suggest are Larkin's proper peers. For Larkin is not alone in the practice of his beholding witness and his capacity for fresh wonder. He wrote in spiritual company with a series of contemporary British poets who also quite consciously seek a healing connection with the familiar world outside the self. While it is certain that Larkin has been influenced by the attitudes and some of the craft strategies of the Movement group of writers, it is worth also taking notice of the way in which his achievement as I have defined and appreciated it exists in the midst of one of the more positive traditions of poetry of the post-war period. It is a tradition which has at its centre a beholding curiosity, and its practitioners are not only partly Lawrence- and Imagist-inspired; they are, as many would agree, among the most accomplished poets writing today. They are peers of Larkin because of the vigour of their art, and because of their participation with him in a tradition of writing that has at the centre of its aesthetic an open, explorative and observant temperament.

7 Larkin's Proper Peers

It is one of the more remarkable aspects of much contemporary poetry in the English tradition that it is a poetry 'empirical in its attitude to all that comes' in a sense wider than Robert Conquest first imagined when he described the Movement poets as such in *New Lines* (1956) almost three decades ago. There is something of a renaissance of the kind of poetry Larkin wrote, a poetry which emerges out of reservations about the obscurity of the Modernist masterpieces and had a desire to craft an art which is written from the perspective of the attending consciousness. While the imagist impulse of the Modernist tradition is gaining new status as stimulus to much contemporary writing, the more subjectively internal, more privately symbolic achievements of the Modernists are being reassessed by contemporary practitioners, and the middle tradition of English poetry can be said once again to own a centrality of status for the artist.

We have already heard Larkin's reasoning on these matters, and his views could even be said to account for the taste he exhibits in the selections which make up his edition of *The Oxford Book of Twentieth Century Verse* (1973). Thom Gunn speaks for many contemporaries, I think, when he writes,

> The only assumption shared by the poets who have emerged in the last ten years is that they do not want to continue the revolution inaugurated by Pound and finally made respectable by learned commentaries on *The Four Quartets*. Yet nobody has pretended that, once the revolution was abandoned, it was possible simply to take up where Hardy left off, as if the experiments of Pound and Eliot had never taken place. Clearly we must, without embodying the revolution, attempt to benefit from it, to understand its causes and study its mistakes.

Gunn insists that contemporary poets have much to learn from the Imagist aspect of the revolution and he admires the Imagists

talent for 'exact delineation of the external world', noting that in
the poetry of real observation there is always the possibility of a
'health howsoever brief'[1] which follows on the transcendence of
confinement in the self. To use a phrase from one of Gunn's own
poems, this fresh attention to 'the world's bare surface'[2] is an
emphatic one in his own more recent volumes. Ted Hughes and
R. S. Thomas, too, are poets remarkable in their empirical
explorations, their desire to connect anew with the mysterious
presence of the immediate world. All three of these poets are
radically different from Larkin on a whole series of counts, but
they nevertheless share with him the rudimentary pleasure of
participation in reality of which the previous pages have been
taking note. For Hughes, Gunn and Thomas, as for Larkin, 'The
greatest poverty / Is not to live in the physical world'.[3]

Among the poets who write in this tradition we could arguably
include such figures as Elizabeth Jennings, Charles Tomlinson
and Seamus Heaney, all of whom take their deepest social and
existential concerns outward to their witness of the living,
palpably present world. But to examine their work here would
distract me from my main purpose of simply drawing attention to
the tradition, and placing Larkin within it as a poet who has peers
other than those commonly referred to by most literary critics.
The similarities which tighten the connection between Larkin,
Hughes, Gunn and Thomas also lie in their shared concern – at
times amounting to an obsession – with a sense of mystery in
reality which they assert as a value in itself. All poets of tense
ambiguity in matters of religion, they nevertheless write a poetry
of impermanent wonder which is valuable from several points of
view. Each of these poets emphasises a different aspect of reality,
but they are united in their common capacity for a responsiveness
to mystery which is both tough-minded and explorative at the
same time. Given such an aware sensibility, they move, it seems
to me, marginally past the sunlessness of a great deal of the
wasteland literature of this century, and past the literature of
despair of our own day. In short, like Larkin, these other poets of
the immediate world address the doubts and spiritual tensions of
their age with a return to 'the world's bare surface' in the hope of
healing the tragic imbalance between mind and reality which
characterises so much of the literature of the modern period.

There is nothing soft about these poets, and their only certain
act of faith thus far consists in faith in a value connected with their

openness to witness, their conviction that there is paradoxically an anxious yet mysterious reality which beckons for enactment in words. In his 'Human Condition' Gunn says, 'Particular, I must / Find out the limitation / Of mind and universe', and

> I seek, to break, my span.
> I am my one touchstone.
> This is a test more hard
> Than any ever known.[4]

The poets in this tradition all 'seek, to break' that 'span', to transcend meaningless subjectivism and behold in the living world an intelligibility redemptive of intellectual and spiritual hope. Like Larkin, they seek to realise moments of illumination which suffice as a temporary, but perhaps also accumulating, answer to the meaninglessness by which their culture and their age is constantly threatened. While they are not reconciled or atoned artists, they are unwilling to give in to easy despair, despite the often intruding attractiveness of that conventional option. All of these writers have a capability for affirmation which is continually rewarded by the flashes of light from the real world which they perceive amidst the surrounding darkness of their time.

Ted Hughes's poetry is animated by a living consciousness of the physical world. His special talent as a poet of this kind consists in his repeatedly compensated curiosity about the instinctually energetic, natural and elemental aspects of reality. Hughes shares with D. H. Lawrence the conviction that the realm of abstraction is stale by comparison to blood-consciousness, the deep and quick mystery of the living cosmos. Hughes renders as alive everything he looks at, from the smallest of creatures to the physical universe imagined as a pulsating whole. He has a superficial reputation for being a poet of the strong will, in spite of the fact that his own comments on poetry endorse a beholding respect for the otherness of the surrounding world. Hughes is certainly an ostensibly more energetic writer than is Larkin, but in his shared pleasure in the mystery of living reality he maintains, along with Larkin, the example of Lawrence as a considerable presence in contemporary poetry.

Natural energy animates Hughes's poems to the extent that they often take on an uncanny life of their own, are enlivened with the flash of instinct, the quick move of surviving nature. As a result, the poems are sometimes considered by his critics and reviewers to be merely violent and prurient. But, if we listen to the teller and not his critics, there is an aspect of his animal poems which Hughes himself points to as in itself healthy – and this is involved in the very process of writing the animal poem. In his *Poetry in the Making* (1967) he says, 'Maybe my concern has been to capture not animals particularly and not poems, but simply things which have a vivid life of their own',[5] and in his advice to schoolchildren on how to write animal poems he advises, 'The one thing is, imagine what you are writing about. See it and live it. Do not think it up laboriously, as if you were working out mental arithmetic. Just look at it, touch it, smell it, listen to it, turn yourself into it.' He goes on to say that if the poet does this the craft of the work almost takes care of itself, and 'You will read back through what you have written and you will get a shock. You will have captured a spirit, a creature.'[6]

The advice which Hughes gives the aspiring poet, the stress he puts on the need to go past the ego to the object in an intimate way, is borne out as accomplished fact in his own poetry:

> His stride is wilderness of freedom:
> The world rolls under the long thrust of his heel.
> Over the cage floor the horizons come.

('The Jaguar'[7])

> Pike, three inches long, perfect
> Pike in all parts, green and tigering the gold.
> Killers from the egg: the malevolent aged grin.
> They dance on the surface among the flies.
>
> Or move, stunned by their own grandeur,
> Over a bed of emerald, silhouette
> Of submarine delicacy and horror,
> A hundred feet long in their world.

('Pike'[8])

The briefest of quotations testify to his ability to capture 'a spirit, a creature'. In the above lines the speaker's perspective is from within the dramatic inscape of the creature itself, is written out of a gift for capturing mystery as fact rather than as idea intrusively searching for supporting symbol. 'Bull Moses', to cite but one of literally hundreds of poems of a similar order, is perhaps one of his finest achieved examples of this ability.

In 'Bull Moses' the speaker looks into a barn, into a 'Blaze of darkness' toward the bull, which he sees in 'a sudden shut-eyed look / Backward into the head'. He registers a quick and sharp moment of meaning: 'Blackness is depth / Beyond star'. In that moment, he welds the deep mystery of the bull's primitive being with that of his own dark recesses of mind, and also with the ramifying and dark eternity past the stars. The visual dimension of 'Bull Moses' re-creates the intractable weight and largeness of the creature, and ends with the poet seeing in the mysterious bull

> something
> Deliberate in his leisure, some beheld future
> Founding in his quiet.
>
> I kept the door wide,
> Closed it after him and pushed the bolt.[9]

'Bull Moses' moves from a moment of primitive fright, through a sense of passing wonder, to the partly humorous reverence of the close. The dark wonderment, in its concomitant sense of awe and shudder at the thick void, is more quietly uncovered in Larkin's conclusion to 'High Windows', where the emptiness startles the poet into a recognition of something obscurely profound which cannot be easily measured into myth, compelling as it might be at the same time. Both Larkin and Hughes are satisfied to leave the moment in all of its ambiguity, merely to re-create it as an enacted miracle of logic.

Hughes's moments of wonder arise naturally out of his observation of the primitive aspects of being. A bull is a bull in Hughes's world and the meaning of his creatures lies mainly in their presence as elemental beings. His more negative critics have distracted us from this effect in his work and have chosen to discuss such things as the nihilism of his poetry, and the nihilism of his 'Crow' persona most especially. But Hughes's Crow, rather than being a nihilistic projection of Hughes himself, 'flying the black flag of himself',[10] is ironically a vibrantly creative force.

In the universe of *Crow* (1971), Crow is energetic, certainly humorous, and above all an agitant, an agent of perception who pesters the issues of Creation. He shocks the reader into attending to the universe from a vital and cosmic perspective. Hence,

> Crow saw the herded mountains, steaming in the morning.
> And he saw the sea
> Dark-spined, with the whole earth in its coils.
> He saw the stars, fuming away into the black, mushrooms of the
>   nothing forest, clouding their spores, the virus of God.
> And he shivered with the horror of Creation.[11]

The thunderous evocation of the universe here is fresh and startling. Although the realisation of the 'stars' as 'mushrooms of / the nothing forest' is an unsettling image, the effect of the lines is to awaken the imagination to its elemental home. Hughes's Crow flies directly out of the primeval night of Shakespeare's *Macbeth* ('Light thickens and the crow / Makes wing to the rooky wood'[12]), and thereby takes on a provocative, almost religious dimension. Hughes has remarked that the 'whole art of writing is to make your reader's imagination go into action',[13] and the Crow poems manage that effect. Hughes's poetry, like Larkin's, invites the reader to participate in the living moment of the universe.

We have seen that the price Larkin has paid in the critical world for tuning up unsettling moments of illumination is an unjust one, given that these moments are in themselves credible, are qualified also by his moments of beautification, and serve as well to give a further maturity to his honesty as a contemporary mind. And as a similarly explorative and open sensibility, Hughes is also in danger of being mistaken as only or primarily a poet of the void. But, if Hughes entertains an existentially horrifying prospect for meaning in *Crow*, a dark mysticism, it is also an exploration which must be placed in balance with his more positive discoveries. Like Larkin, Hughes is a poet of agnostic wonder, so, while there are registrations of spiritual shock in his chronicle of moments, there are also some of compelling light. There are some of revitalising mystery, and of pleasure in that mystery.

The usual dimension of the Hughes poem includes the basic wisdom of Lawrence's sense of the cosmos as a mysterious presence. This gives to his work a power which leaves critical exegesis, I think, always running behind. There is pleasure in the evocation of the world in Hughes's work, and that spiritual and artistic delight is almost always more basic than particular themes his individual poems might also convey. 'Wind' is a striking case in point. In the context of this poem, we sense the pleasure in reality which late Imagist theorists such as Wallace Stevens felt is vital to the sustenance of elemental spiritual bearings.

This house has been far out at sea all night,
The woods crashing through darkness, the booming hills,
Winds stampeding the fields under the window
Floundering black astride and blinding wet

Till day rose; then under an orange sky
The hills had new places, and wind wielded
Blade-like, luminous black and emerald,
Flexing like the lens of a mad eye.

At noon I scaled along the house-side as far as
The coal-house door. I dared once to look up –
Through the brunt wind that dented the balls of my eyes
The tent of the hills drummed and strained its guyrope,

The fields quivering, the skyline a grimace,
At any second to bang and vanish with a flap:
The wind flung a magpie away and a black-
Back gull bent like an iron bar slowly. The house

Rang like some fine green goblet in the note
That any second would shatter it. Now deep
In chairs, in front of the great fire, we grip
Our hearts and cannot entertain book, thought,

Or each other. We watch the fire blazing,
And feel the roots of the house move, but sit on,
Seeing the window tremble to come in,
Hearing the stones cry out under the horizon.[14]

The strong actuality of 'Wind', and its presentation of the landscape in convulsion, gives it a stark immediacy which makes the fact of the event inseparable from the idea it discovers in its naturally symbolic motion. Hughes has said, 'In writing that poem I was mainly concerned with the strength of the blast, the way it seems to shake the world up like a box of toys.'[15] And, because of this initially mimetic intention, the poem's theme rises inevitably from its observed setting and takes pleasure in its feeling for reality. The artifice of the poem is in its diction, its appropriately strong verbs, for instance, and in its enjambed syntax, a syntax that mimes the action of the wind itself. The ravelled landscape and the endangered buildings stand as natural symbols of the fragility of human creations in the midst of elemental forces. The wind's 'cry[ing] out under the horizon' presents both the whistle of the wind's intensity and its primitive hold on the sub-civilised aspects of being. The animated observation of the poem beholds humanity's tenuous grip on existence. That precariousness is symbolically evoked in the figure who scales along the house to the coal-house door, and in the creation of the figures around the fire in a huddle which is evocative of primitive ancestors hiding in a cave, away from the blast of nature.

We are used to this kind of elemental pleasure in Larkin's more solitary poems, such as 'Livings' and 'Sad Steps', and in his many works which juxtapose the vitality of the physical universe with the confinement of social life. When Hughes speaks of the value of these moments when nature is witnessed afresh, he clearly states their worth in terms which Larkin would comprehend. Thinking of the value of elemental witness Hughes says,

> Civilization is comparatively new, it is still a bit of a strain on our nerves – it is not quite a home to mankind yet, we still need occasional holidays back in the old surroundings. It is only there that the ancient instincts and feelings in which most of our body lives can feel at home and on their own ground. It is almost as though these places were generators where we can recharge our run-down batteries. And what do we recharge with, what sort of electricity? Those prehistoric feelings, satisfactions we are hardly aware of except as a sensation of pleasure – these are like a blood transfusion to us, and in wild surroundings they rise to the surface and refresh us, renew us. For some people, even to think about such places is a refreshment.[16]

What for many is only the terrifying, the dreadful without

spiritual dividends, is for Hughes and Larkin a source of spiritual revitalisation. As is also the case in Larkin, Hughes finds both awe and beauty in his participation in the natural world. For Hughes, the greatness of poetry lies in its special task of expressing what he has termed 'Something of the spirit of the snowflake in the water of the river. Something of the duplicity and relativity and merely fleeting quality of all this. Something of the almighty importance of it and something of the utter meaninglessness.'[17] Here he indicates the ambiguity of his wonder, his openness to exploration, and his unwillingness to nail down his pleasure and his dread into a controlling mythology.

And there is nothing in Hughes's comments on poetry, or in the poetry itself, which will satisfy the nailing-down instincts of the critic. In Hughes's chronicle there is (as yet) insufficient evidence with which to conclude a case for either the imbecility of Creation or its ultimate harmony. Starting with an empirical strategy of the imagination, and a recognition of the possibility of meaning in the physical world, he remains, at the height of his powers, a poet of passing wonder. At the very least, in these matters he achieves that 'health howsoever brief' of which Gunn speaks and which Larkin congruently values in spite of his 'less deceived' identity as a poet.

Thom Gunn and Ted Hughes are the two poets in the tradition of this kind of poetry who are most often compared, but for different reasons from those I am interested in here. Their reputation for celebrating the human will, for what Patrick Swinden calls in Gunn 'a sort of poetic thuggery',[18] gives, perhaps, a kind of logic to Faber and Faber's publication of a combined selection of their work. None the less, Gunn's poetry has gone through a significant change in emphasis in the past twenty years, and there is as part of that change a notable shift in his work away from the early 'thuggery' and toward a poetry of the physical world. Gunn's reputation for a thematic concern with subjective will and self-absorption has too easily distracted his critics from this shift toward an essentially Lawrentian and Imagist poetry of beholding observation.

Of his early *Fighting Terms* (1954) Gunn said in 1964, 'there is very little in it that I particularly want to keep',[19] and he cast that volume as immature. Moving away from studies in sheer will, he has come to recognise the healing otherness of outward reality, and that shift is nascent in his reviews in the *Yale Review*. A review article he wrote in 1964 and from which I have already quoted is particularly informative in this regard, as it seems to preface the more empirically based poetry he has been writing for the past twenty years.

That article ranges across the work of five contemporary poets while addressing the question of the contemporary value of the Modernist experiment in the arts. Gunn underlines as the single strength of the experiment a health he associates with the aspect of it which has its theoretical roots in the Imagist tradition, namely the concern for the 'exact delineation of the external world'. Yet, very like Larkin, Gunn is not simply influenced by that tradition and he has elsewhere remarked that 'I certainly don't want to be like Robert Bly, who is writing purely in terms of particulars, and I don't want to be an Imagist which is something rather close.'[20] Like Larkin, Gunn is a poet of both image and expression, and it is the example of Imagist attendance to reality which he extracts but modifies toward fuller statement.

This growing interest in the careful re-creation of the real world has noticeable effects in Gunn's more recent volumes. In *Moly* (1971) and *Jack Straw's Castle* (1976), Gunn moves into a habit of imaginative participation in the real world as a way of experiencing that 'health howsoever brief' which assuages his uncertainties as an existential poet. In both volumes he attempts to transcend his established, customary self and spiritually break the 'span' of which he spoke in 'Human Condition' by employing a precept he once attributed to Albert Camus: that 'the attempt to look outwards is more important than expression of the self'.[21] The title poem of *Moly* is important in this regard. The swine–man persona searches for his humanity in nature by seeking the magic herb:

> I root and root, you think that it is greed,
> It is, but I seek out a plant I need.
>
> Direct me gods, whose changes are holy
> To where it flickers deep in grass, the moly:
>
> Cool flesh of magic in each leaf and shoot,
> From the milk flower to the black forked root.

From this fat dungeon I could rise to skin
And human title, putting pig within.

I push my big grey wet snout through the green,
Dreaming the flower I have never seen.[22]

'Moly' is a pivotal poem in Gunn's chronicle, central because of its
expressed desire for a healing connection with the physical world.
Some have regarded the metaphor of the moly as primarily a
reference to Gunn's interest in drug culture, but it is also
significant, I think, that the 'flower' referred to here becomes the
sun in the poem 'Sunlight', which ends the volume on a note of
celebration and praise. A moment of healing does take place in
Moly and it is the result of a receptivity in the poet to the living
presence of the real world. 'Sunlight', is thus akin in spirit to
Larkin's 'Solar'.

Some things, by their affinity light's token,
Are more than shown: steel glitters from a track;
Small glittering scoops, after a wave has broken,
Dimple the water in its draining back;

Water, glass, metal, match light in their raptures,
Flashing their many answers to the one.
What captures light belongs to what it captures:
The whole side of a world facing the sun,

Re-turned to woo the original perfection,
Giving itself to what created it,
And wearing green in sign of its subjection.
It is as if the sun were infinite.

But angry flaws are swallowed by the distance;
It varies, moves, its concentrated fires
Are slowly dying – the image of persistence
Is an image, only, of our own desires:

Desires and knowledge touch without relating.
The system of which sun and we are part
Is both imperfect and deteriorating.
And yet the sun outlasts us at the heart.

> Great seedbed, yellow centre of the flower,
> Flower on its own, without root or stem,
> Giving all colour and all shape their power,
> Still recreating in defining them,
>
> Enable us, altering like you, to enter
> Your passionless love, impartial but intense,
> And kindle in acceptance round your centre,
> Petals of light lost in your innocence.[23]

'Sunlight' is very contemporary, factual, in its knowledge that the sun is limited as metaphor. The sun is part of a universe which is 'both imperfect and deteriorating'. The picture of the sun's relation to earth in the first three stanzas is a nostalgic one, and the poet knows this even while he is engaged by the beauty of the portrayal. The next two stanzas exist as an antithetical motion, betraying the more poetic view of the universe the previous stanzas embody. Yet, despite the potentially crippling scepticism in the knowledge expressed in the middle stanzas, a moment of at-oneness is none the less savoured and recorded. The wonder is of a familiarly passing order, but in any event it survives as an epiphany of hope in Gunn's chronicle. There is a Lawrentian desire for a healing organic connection with the universe in this poem, a desire to recover a sense of the cosmos as relative to the human being in an intimate way.

As in Larkin's and Hughes's analogous explorations, there is no nailing-down of the moment into myth or established religion. The momentary connection with the universe is let alone as something of value in itself, as pleasant to the imagination, yet not requiring that the poet delude himself about its absolute significance. Gunn's wish to participate in the presence of the sun makes for a moment of epiphany that avoids abstractions which might dilute the healing-effect. The wonder is fleeting but the poet, impelled to preserve it, records it all the same. The result is, in the context of Gunn's chronicle, a poem that has the brilliance of a flash of light when set against much earlier, more despondent poems such as 'The Annihilation of Nothing', where

> It is despair that nothing cannot be
> Flares in the mind and leaves a smoky mark
> Of dread.

> Look upward. Neither firm nor free,
> Purposeless matter hovers in the dark.[24]

Gunn's development as a poet is to a large extent chartable as a move past just such despondency at the prospect of the physical world as meaningless physics. Instead, in his more recent poetry there is a Lawrentian and Imagist prizing of momentary connections with the otherness of the real world.

A willingness to attend wholly to the world that surrounds him continues in Gunn's *Jack Straw's Castle*. As a volume it is varied in its themes, and they range from a preoccupation with Californian drug culture to the turmoils of mental subjectivism. Many of the poems are, as Derwent May says, about the 'lightness and balance of the body',[25] or, one synonymously adds, have a Lawrentian esteem for all forms of organic connection with being. In 'Diagrams', for instance, there is a moment of praise which rises, Larkin-like, from the ostensibly unpromising details of the ordinary urban world:

> Downtown, an office tower is going up.
> And from the mesa of the unfinished top
> Big cranes jut, spectral points of stiffened net:
> Angled top-heavy artifacts, and yet
> Diagrams from the sky, as if its air
> Could drop lines, snip them off, and leave them there.
>
> On girders round them, Indians pad like cats,
> With wrenches in their pockets and hard hats.
>
> They wear their yellow boots like moccasins,
> Balanced where air ends and where steel begins,
> Sky men, and through the sole's flesh, chewed and pliant,
> They feel the studded bone-edge of the giant.
> It grunts and sways through its whole metal length.
> And giving to the air is sign of strength.[26]

In its appreciation of the harmony between the agile workers and the supple girders, 'Diagrams' finds a prosaic at-oneness which is moved into the realm of the poetic. In this poem, and in another in the volume, 'Iron Landscapes (and the Statue of Liberty)', where Gunn says, 'I'm at peace with the iron landscape too',[27] he opens his imagination in witnessing consent to the industrialised landscape precisely because it is a human landscape after all, the reality in which we live, and one that is not without traces of beauty.

The apotheosis of Gunn's participation in outer reality comes in *Jack Straw's Castle* in the long, four-part poem 'The Geysers'. Throughout 'The Geysers' the speaker observes a harmony suggested by the bathers and hot-springs locale; and in the final section, 'The Bath House', in an opening into appropriate free verse form, he re-creates the spiritual–sensual release which the moment of witness gives forth:

> I yielded
>   oh, the yield
>   what have I slept?
> my blood is yours the hands that take accept
> . . .
> torn from the self
>   in which I breathed and trod
> I am
>   I am raw meat
>   I am a god.[28]

This might disperse literally and figuratively as so much hot air were it not for the fact that the entire poem moves slowly and gradually toward a state of being 'torn from the self' all along. The transcendence, that is, is nourished by and is dependent on the speaker's ability to remain openly attendant, empirically reverent, to everything which surrounds him. The second section, 'The Cool Stream', is for instance an evocation of a bathing-scene which, in its visual celebration of detail and grasp of unconscious ritual harmony, is reminiscent of Larkin's 'To the Sea'. Like Larkin's poem, it finds a 'health howsoever brief' in the pleasure of participating observation. 'The Cool Stream' celebrates a human and a topographical scene, and its last stanza is paradigmatic of its appreciative and beholding glance:

> And some are trying to straddle a floating log,
> Some rest and pass a joint, some climb the fall:
> Tan black and pink, firm shining bodies, all
> Move with a special unconsidered grace.

> For though we have invaded this glittering place
> And broke the silences, yet we submit:
> So wholly, we are details of it.[29]

Self-consciousness is replaced by an intimacy of connection with the living reality. Earlier, the speaker notices a snake which rears its head from the water. In noting it he says, 'Tongue-flicker, and a fly has disappeared. / What elegance! it does not watch itself.'[30] Subjective consciousness, inward-gazing self-consciousness, is analysed here and throughout *Jack Straw's Castle* and is seen as a destructive habit of mind. Beholding observation of the real world is, on the other hand, recognised as partly an antidote to that malady. The beholding glance is a revitalising source of imaginative and intellectual pleasure; and at its best it includes the sensation of harmony with all other being which is there in the lines from 'The Cool Stream' cited above. As with Larkin, in Gunn there is a quality of mysticism in all of this which stays close to the literal plane of reality and also is careful not to overstate its implications in absolutes.

Gunn is a poet of existential doubts and spiritual tensions, and as such he is a poet whose experiences of light do not invariably and/or quaintly erase his qualms about the essential ignorance of man in his 'human condition'. Nevertheless, like other poets of the physical world, he has reached a hopeful juncture where the world exists before him as potentially regenerative in its provocation of pleasure and intellectual surprise. He is an anxious poet, as are Larkin's other proper peers, but like them he guards his anxiety with an experiential alertness that has given new life to his chronicle of epiphanies. In 'A Snow Vision', after the speaker dramatises a violent storm, he concludes,

> It ends. I open my eyes to snow.
> I can sleep now; as I drowse I know
>
> I must keep to the world's bare surface,
> I must perceive, and perceive what is:
>
> for though the hold of perception must
> harden but diminish, like the frost,
>
> yet still there may be something retained
> against the inevitable end.[31]

This keeping 'to the world's bare surface' amounts to the agnostic wonder we are used to in Larkin's volumes. It does not provide a ready answer to the doubts of the feeling personality in the contemporary age, but its explorative openness gives to it a vigour of religious intensity which could be said to precede absolutes and at the same time surpasses the fatigue of more traditional, mythic poetry.

Bringing R. S. Thomas into the discussion at this point might at first appear to be a simple about-face, in the sense that Thomas is one of the more myth-oriented (read 'traditionally religious') poets of our age – and therefore unsympathetic to a kind of poetry which substitutes wonder at outward reality for established religion. But there is a difference between Thomas's employment of traditional myth and that of, say, John Milton or T. S. Eliot. And it is hinted at by John Press when he says that 'Thomas' faith is rooted in the soil of Wales, and also in the earth, which is our element, our planet, our home.'[32] As a more visibly mythical poet than Larkin, Hughes or Gunn, Thomas is certainly very different from them, but he is also unexpectedly similar to them in that the very basis of his work lies in its revitalising pleasure in the presence of the physical world. That pleasure in Thomas not only serves as a rejuvenating force in his own particular concerns as a religious poet who seeks to renew old mythology, but also exists in his work as the imaginative salve to his doubts and concerns as a poet of pain and moral indignation.

Thomas's effects as a poet of wonder are never achieved in the merely abstract. Press has appropriately praised the physicality of the poet's style and its characteristic 'harshness and pungency of concept and phrase'; it is as though Thomas were always 'paring away the surplus flesh of epithet and of explanation, stripping the language to the bone'.[33] The accuracy of this praise is borne out in the poetry itself and also in Thomas's view of poetry as we overhear him express it in the title poem of *Poetry for Supper* (1967), written four years after Press's appreciation. In that poem, Thomas presents in dialogue form the tension he perceives between the physical world and the poet's urge toward artifice:

> 'Listen, now, verse should be as natural
> As the small tuber that feeds on muck
> And grows slowly from obtuse soil
> To the white flower of immortal beauty.'

'Natural, hell! What was it Chaucer
Said once about the long toil
That goes like blood to the poem's making?
Leave it to nature and the verse sprawls,
Limp as bindweed, if it break at all
Life's iron crust. Man, you must sweat
And rhyme your guts taut, if you'd build
Your verse a ladder.'

                        'You speak as though
No sunlight ever surprised the mind
Groping on its cloudy path.'

'Sunlight's a thing that needs a window
Before it enter a dark room.
Windows don't happen.'

                     So two old poets,
Hunched at their beer in the low haze
Of an inn parlour, while the talk ran
Noisily by them, glib with prose.[34]

Thomas resolves the tension in his own poetry toward the precarious middle of the dialectic. He manages to capture the 'sunlight' which seems to surprise 'the mind / Groping on its cloudy path', even though this is an effect in his poetry which we can appreciate only because he also crafts the 'window'. And the window he provides is often, in its clarity, an imagist one, both in its close attention to the details of the physical world and in its care to frame moments of discovered illumination.

Hence, 'A Peasant' is a typical early Thomas poem in that its strategy of discovery is outward to the living world and that motion of consciousness is rewarded with the surprise of light. A perception of the horrifying vacancy latent in Welsh rural life leads the speaker toward a feeling of spiritual emptiness and fright; but that initial observation is amended in the concluding image of the poem. 'A Peasant' ends with a telescoped image which has a placing-effect and it surfaces on the page with the flash of surprise of which 'Poetry for Supper' speaks. Thomas says of the peasant,

There is something frightening in the vacancy of his mind.
His clothes, sour with years of sweat
And animal contact, shock the refined,
But affected, sense with their stark naturalness.
Yet this is your prototype, who, season by season
Against siege of rain and the wind's attrition,
Preserves his stock an impregnable fortress
Not to be stormed, even in death's confusion.
Remember him, then, for he, too, is a winner of wars,
Enduring like a tree under the curious stars.[35]

There is a Lawrentian immediacy and an Imagist concentration in these lines, and, in his careful comingling of the physical world and the expressive dimension of the poem, Thomas demonstrates that his poetic consciousness is of the order of ambiguous wonder found in the work of Larkin, Hughes and Gunn alike. In the sudden, ascending picture of the peasant as 'Enduring like a tree under the curious stars', Thomas's effect is akin to Larkin's passing wonder in such poems as 'The Whitsun Weddings', where the close of the poem turns rapidly upward in a rushing image of human mystery. In both instances an appreciation of the beauty and mystery of ordinary humanity is stated after an initial boredom, and abstract distance is subdued in the name of a further attention to reality.

'Lowri Dafydd' is also reminiscent of the Imagists, and it recalls the kind of sensitivity Pound managed in 'The River-Merchant's Wife: A Letter':

> My name is Lowri Dafydd;
> Famous for nursing I was.
> I rode pillion on a winged horse
> Through the high passes of cloud
> To come to a queen's palace.
> Airy fingers undid the knot
> In time's stubborn bandage
> About my green eyes.
> Who knows how long I stayed?
> My pay was the sweet talk
> In sun-dusted rooms
> Of folk, busy as flowers,
> Praising my hands' skill.

When I returned, stars were out
Over my roof, the door fallen
About its hinges, and on the hearth
A cold wind blowing for ever.[36]

The imagistic base of English poetry is alive and well in Thomas's work, and the physicality of the descending lines of the above poem is a measure of his visual brilliance as a poet. Those lines, in their naturally symbolic effects, perfectly match Larkin's insistence on the need for the poet to remain close to the familiar world. The physical world as it manifests itself on the sensitive consciousness, adjusting the concepts of that consciousness with fresh insight, is at the centre of Thomas's achievement as a poet, for all of his simultaneous obsession with the contour and details of traditional religious mythology.

In the poetry which Thomas has written in approximately the past decade – that, for instance, of his volume *H'm* (1971) – the poet moves from his usual theme of rural Welsh life to a more energetic treatment of his religious concerns. The new energy is there as a shift from his concerns as a parish priest to a more cosmic dimension as a poet of the living and the poetic universe. Thomas has always been a poet of doubt, and his early piece 'In Church' is one which captures this kind of spiritual ambiguity in its framing of a pestered believer who sits in a dark church, 'testing his faith / On emptiness, nailing his questions / One by one to an untenanted cross'.[37] The drama of Thomas's doubt takes place on a larger physical stage in *H'm*. That stage is the entire cosmos, and as such it shares with Hughes's *Crow* a dimension of dread and awe which links these otherwise very dissimilar poets by their common perspective. *H'm*, and others of Thomas's volumes of the past decade, share with Hughes's elemental poetry an unsettled quality and a preoccupation with the way in which mythology emerges from the topographical plane of the universe. Thomas shares with Hughes a willingness to explore this relationship with an open eye. He is quite willing to expel all forms and details of myth which do not match the experiential fact of the world.

Like Hughes and Larkin, Thomas takes his concerns as a religious poet to the out-of-doors. Because he is not just nostalgic for traditional religious certainty, like Larkin, but has a strong desire to animate that mythology again, he seeks to place that mythology in a new light amidst the concerns of contemporary culture. This gives to his work a sense of urgency and a weightiness which goes far past the institutional torpor of Larkin's depiction of religion in 'Aubade', for instance. Thomas is a poet who deals with religious myth, but explores its relevance to reality. So, in 'Making', for example, there is an attempt to breathe fresh life into Genesis:

> And having built it
> I set about finishing it
> To my taste: first moss, then grass
> Annually renewed, and animals
> To divert me: faces stared in
> From the wild. I thought up the flowers
> Then birds. I found the bacteria
> Sheltering in primordial
> Darkness and called them forth
> To the light. Quickly the earth
> Teemed. Yet still an absence
> Disturbed me. I slept and dreamed
> Of a likeness, fashioning it,
> When I woke, to a slow
> Music; in love with it
> For itself, giving it freedom
> To love me; risking the disappointment.[38]

Thomas's gift for dramatising the Creation myth gives to *H'm* a zest of existential suddenness of similar effect to that expressed by Larkin and Hughes. The enjambed sharpness of 'Quickly the earth / Teemed' is characteristic of *H'm* in its surprising sense of the presence of the universe. This particular poem is relatively quiet in tone and manages a graceful effect in its closing lines. But *H'm* contains many troubled pieces, many that house the doubt so central to the paridigmatic early poem 'In Church'. In 'Via Negativa', for instance, God is seen as He who 'keeps the interstices / In our knowledge, the darkness / Between stars'.[39] In that poem God is conceived of as an absence, an incompletion we search for in vain. And in 'Soliloquy' God is configured as a violent, Old Testament avenger who looks down on a now materialistic, machine-worshipping Creation and decides to erase his error – to poison his failed experiment with 'invisible / Viruses'.[40] The viruses could be as general as pollution, eco-catastrophe, or as specific as cancer. Each poem in *H'm* is an intensely explorative attempt to relate Godhead to the urgency of contemporary reality. Because of Thomas's willingness to deal with the crises of our day, and because of his concern that traditional mythology – its details and its answers – may be inadequate to the crises, many of the poems in *H'm* express doubt more than atonement. As with Hughes's *Crow*, the cumulative effect of *H'm* provokes in the reader an enlivened sensation of the physical universe, one in which the creatureliness of humanity is stressed amidst debate about the scarcity of compelling mythology.

Thomas's *Frequencies* (1978) exists as another cluster of momentary doubts and momentary epiphanies of light in his religious chronicle of poems. Many of its poems are very dark expressions of existential anxiety. It is, nevertheless, inappropriate to guess where Thomas's spiritual journey will eventually lead him – although one notices tendencies, preferences in his more recent poems. 'The Moon in Lleyn' is worthy of attention on this point. After the first stanza, in which the speaker comes to the conclusion that 'Religion is over', the motion of doubt begins to bring up its opposite. And that contrary motion takes place as the result of hints suggested to the speaker by the actual church he observes in the emerging symbolism of the poem's immediate setting:

> But a voice sounds
> in my ear: Why so fast,
> mortal? These very seas
> are baptized. The parish
> has a saint's name time cannot
> unfrock. In cities that
> have outgrown their promise people
> are becoming pilgrims
> again, if not to this place,
> then to the recreation of it
> in their own spirits. You must remain
> kneeling. Even as this moon
> making its way through the earth's
> cumbersome shadow, prayer, too,
> has its phases.[41]

In several of the poems in *Later Poems: 1972–1982* (1983), a volume which includes the poem above, there are epiphanies of reinforcing hope which would seem to indicate that the poet will always manage to sustain his openness to belief even if that belief must finally require of him a measure of Kierkegaardian existential stress.

And it is in poems such as 'Threshold' that he states that stress perfectly: 'Ah, / what balance is needed at / the edges of such an abyss. / I am alone on the surface / of a turning planet.'[42] The locution recalls Gunn's 'world's bare surface', and it also prefaces, in its spiritual tension, many of Thomas's poems of open wonder and doubt in confrontation with the planet. Thus, while Thomas is a poet of profound doubt, his chronicle to date is rich with many poems which either reassert the vigour of traditional Christian mythology, or recover a sense of mystery in the physical world which helps to keep his hope tenable. In 'Night Sky', originally published in *Frequencies*, he says of the stars,

> What they are saying is
> that there is life there, too;
> that the universe is the size it is
> to enable us to catch up.
>
> They have gone on from the human;
> that shining is a reflection
> of their intelligence. Godhead
> is the colonisation by mind
>
> of untenanted space. It is its own
> light, a statement beyond language
> of conceptual truth. Every night
> is a rinsing myself of the darkness
> that is in my veins. I let the stars inject me
> with fire, silent as it is far,
> but certain in its cauterising
> of my despair. I am a slow
>
> traveller, but there is more than time
> to arrive. Resting in the intervals
> of my breathing, I pick up the signals
> relayed to me from a periphery I comprehend.[43]

Built into Thomas's very figuration here is the metaphor of healing so prominent in the poetry of reality we are used to in Larkin, Gunn and Hughes, fellow members of a tradition of the aesthetic of wonder. Thomas is a poet radically different from Larkin in more ways than I have space to discuss here; but the Larkin of passing wonder who in 'Absences' says, after his evocation of an elemental scene, 'Such attics cleared of me! Such absences!' (*LD*, p. 40) has more in common with the poet who says 'Every night / is a rinsing myself of the darkness / that is in my veins' than those differences might at first lead us to believe. Like Larkin, Hughes and Gunn, Thomas has discovered a meaning in reality which does not easily lead him to absolutes, yet nourishes a 'health howsoever brief' in the form of epiphanies of light.

At its most positive, what is embodied in the kind of poetry these poets write is the recovery in twentieth-century poetry of an awakened attention to the potential for meaning in the plane of the real world. Thomas is the poet of reality who more usually seeks to name God in his works, and traditional mythology is more prominent in his chronicle than in the works of Larkin, Hughes and Gunn. But, this notwithstanding, he in large measure speaks for the entire tradition, I think, when in 'Emerging' he says,

> We are beginning to see
> now it is matter is the scaffolding
> of spirit; that the poem emerges
> from the morphemes and phonemes; that
> as form in sculpture is the prisoner
> of the hard rock, so in everyday life
> it is the plain facts and natural happenings
> that conceal God and reveal him to us
> little by little under the mind's tooling.[44]

Thomas perhaps makes God more explicit here than the other poets in the tradition would prefer. However, in his recognition of the return of a sense of mystery to the poet's consciousness he states a difference of attention which characterises the poetry of contemporary wonder, and marks it off from the wasteland tradition of this century.

Nearly three decades ago D. J. Enright expressed an unconventional concern that Modernism had created a continuing tradition of poetry that embodies an obsessive cynicism, a nihilism, and he charged that the despair at its centre is ignorant of the wider truth – and therefore narrow in its spiritual approach to experience. When he formulated a more hopeful aesthetic for the poets who would write in the post-war period, he described this 'new' poetry in the form of a conjecture about its future practitioners:

> Their poetry, I believe, is likely to be 'disenchanted' – not a poetry of disillusionment so much as a poetry without illusions: a poetry of realism, but careful, thoughtful and measured realism, and not a poetry of mere squalor. Not, like Eliot's, the work of a man who has accepted the Fall and all its implications, but certainly the work of a chastened man who sees his species in danger of physical extinction and speaks of what is worthy to be spoken of before the end comes. I suspect that the role of the contemporary poet is not, as Eliot saw it, to make men realize their spiritual shabbiness – nor, as with the Georgians, to pat them on the back and cheer them up – but, rather, to dissuade mankind from committing suicide. This strikes me as a reasonably important role, and it is hoped that our poets – the poets of all countries – will prove adequate to it. [45]

Larkin and his peers, in their poetry of beholding wonder, fulfil Enright's projection in abundant detail. All these poets are, in their different ways, veterans of the darkness. And it is because of this that such hope as exists in their volumes is undoubtedly the more trustworthy – purely optimistic writing has, somehow, a hollow ring to it in our age. These poets do not recover the mythic vigour of the Romantic poets, and they certainly do not resolve their explorations with a Georgian retrenchment into traditional pieties. What they manage instead is a recovery of a middle disposition next to reality, and an attitude which connects their work with the mystery of reality as we see it in the poetry of both the past and the modern period.

It is in the works of Larkin and his peers that the curious spirit reasserts itself in spite of the wasteland heritage of much of the writing in this century. What Thomas names 'everyday life' and those 'plain facts and natural happenings' is the base from which they start. And if poets can still be said to be the antennae of the race, this poetry of openness to the mysterious fact of living reality can be said to have a major importance in our time.

Notes

CHAPTER ONE: INTRODUCTION

1. These publications are: David Timms, *Philip Larkin* (Edinburgh: Oliver and Boyd, 1973); *Phoenix*, nos 11–12 (1973–4), a special issue on Larkin; Lolette Kuby, *An Uncommon Poet for the Common Man: A Study of Philip Larkin* (The Hague and Paris: Mouton, 1974); Alan Brownjohn, *Philip Larkin*, Writers and their Work (London: Longman, for the British Council, 1975); Bruce Martin, *Philip Larkin*, Twayne's English Authors no. 234 (Boston, Mass.: G. K. Hall, 1978); B. C. Bloomfield, *Philip Larkin: A Bibliography, 1933–1976* (London: Faber and Faber, 1979); Simon Petch, *The Art of Philip Larkin*, Sydney Studies in Literature (Sydney: Sydney University Press, 1981); *Larkin at Sixty*, ed. Anthony Thwaite (London, Faber and Faber, 1982); and Andrew Motion, *Philip Larkin*, Contemporary Writers (London and New York: Methuen, 1982).
2. In *Philip Larkin* David Timms relates, 'In a recent (1972) broadcast of tributes to Larkin on his fiftieth birthday, W. H. Auden called him a "master of the English language". Roy Fuller, who, like Auden, has been Professor of Poetry at Oxford, also recorded his admiration of Larkin's work in his broadcast, as did Larkin's distinguished, and very different contemporary, Ted Hughes' (p. 2).

   And the praise does not stop there. In a reply to a question posed to him by Ian Hamilton on the state of poetry in England, Thom Gunn remarked, 'it seems awfully dreary. There are a few totally unconnected people whom I think are very good, Ted Hughes, Donald Davie, and Philip Larkin'. See 'Four Conversations', an interview with Ian Hamilton in *London Magazine*, 4 (Nov 1964) 68. Seamus Heaney has written two appreciative analyses of Larkin's poetry. In one he praises Larkin as a poet of 'composed and tempered English Nationalism'. See 'Now and in England', *Critical Inquiry*, 3 (1977) 486. Heaney's second article is in *Larkin at Sixty*, pp. 131–8, and is titled 'The Main of Light'. John Betjeman wrote an appreciative review of *The Whitsun Weddings*: 'Common Experiences', *Listener*, 19 Mar 1964, p. 483. For Alan Brownjohn's opinion see his *Philip Larkin*, and also his essay 'Novels into Poems', in *Larkin at Sixty*, pp. 109–19. These examples are, of course, selective representations of the esteem in which Larkin is held by established poets. Finally, Robert Lowell spoke for many other poets, I think, when he said, 'When I read Larkin first in 1956, he made other styles obsolete.' See 'Digressions from Larkin's 20th-Century Verse', *Encounter*, 40 (1973) 66–8.

3. Larkin's *Required Writing: Miscellaneous Pieces 1955–1982* (London: Faber and Faber, 1983) was released around the time my study was completed. Because of this, and because Larkin's selection does not contain all his commentaries and interviews, I have quoted him from the original sources when citing his comments on writing.
4. Clive James, 'On his Wit', in *Larkin at Sixty*, pp. 103–4.
5. John Wain, 'The Poetry of Philip Larkin: A Lecture given at Oxford on March 12, 1975', repr. in *Malahat Review*, no. 39 (July 1976) 97.
6. Roger Bowen, 'Poet in Transition: Philip Larkin's *XX Poems*', *Iowa Review*, 8, no. 1 (1977) 87.
7. 'Philip Larkin Praises the Poetry of Thomas Hardy', *Listener*, 25 July 1968, p. 111.
8. See J. R. Watson, 'The Other Larkin', *Critical Quarterly*, 17 (1975) 347–61; Motion's *Philip Larkin*; and Heaney's related article 'The Main of Light', in *Larkin at Sixty*.
9. Philip Larkin, 'Four Conversations', interview with Ian Hamilton, *London Magazine*, 4 (Nov 1964) 72–3.
10. For sensible commentary on Larkin's affinities with Thomas Hardy, see Bibliography for items by C. B. Cox and by Samuel Hynes. On Larkin's affinities with W. H. Auden, see F. W. Bateson, 'Auden's (and Empson's) Heirs', *Essays in Criticism*, 7 (1957) 76–80. The most extensive treatments of Larkin's legacy from W. B. Yeats are in Petch, *The Art of Philip Larkin*, and Motion, *Philip Larkin*. I am unaware of any study which details Larkin's affinities with Louis MacNeice, but the anti-Modernist, directly experiential temper of much of the poetry of the 1930s is strongly present in both Larkin's aesthetic of poetry and his poetry itself.

CHAPTER TWO: POETIC PERSONALITY

1. Philip Larkin, in *Poet's Choice*, ed. Paul Engle and Joseph Langland (New York: The Dial Press, 1962), p. 202.
2. Larkin, in 'Four Conversations', *London Magazine*, 4, 74.
3. Philip Larkin, 'Out of the Air: Not Like Larkin', *Listener*, 17 Aug 1972, p. 209.
4. Philip Larkin, in *Viewpoints: Poets in Conversation with John Haffenden* (London and Boston, Mass.: Faber and Faber, 1981) p. 119. Larkin continues, 'I didn't invent age and death and failure and all that, but how can you ignore them? Hardy or someone said that life was a comedy to those who think, but a tragedy to those who feel. Good stuff' (p. 119).
5. Martin, *Philip Larkin*, p. 13.
6. Philip Larkin, 'Life with a Hole in It', *Poetry Supplement*, compiled by Philip Larkin for the Poetry Book Society (London: Poetry Book Society, 1974) unpaginated.
7. Anthony Thwaite, 'The Poetry of Philip Larkin', in *The Survival of Poetry: A Contemporary Survey*, ed. Martin Dodsworth (London: Faber and Faber, 1970) p. 50.

8. Patrick Swinden, review of *High Windows*, in *Critical Quarterly*, 16 (1974) 281.
9. Larkin, in *Viewpoints*, p. 115.
10. Quoted from a conversation with Philip Oakes. See Oakes's review of *Larkin at Sixty* in *Sunday Times*, 23 May 1982.
11. Alan Bennett, in *Larkin at Sixty*, pp. 69 and 70.
12. Philip Larkin, 'Betjeman En Bloc', review of John Betjeman, *Collected Poems*, in *Listen*, 3 (Spring 1959) 15.
13. Philip Larkin, 'W. H. Auden (1907–1973)', *New Statesman*, 5 Oct 1973, p. 479.
14. Philip Larkin, 'Frivolous and Vulnerable', review of Stevie Smith, *Selected Poems*, in *New Statesman*, 28 Sep 1962, 417.
15. Larkin, in *Viewpoints*, p. 125.
16. Philip Larkin, Introduction to John Betjeman, *Collected Poems*, compiled by the Earl of Birkenhead (Boston, Mass.: Houghton Mifflin, 1971) p. xxxviii.
17. Elizabeth Wordsworth, 'Good and Clever', in *The Oxford Book of Twentieth-Century English Verse*, ed. Philip Larkin (Oxford: Clarendon Press, 1973) p. 26.
18. Philip Larkin, 'Context: Philip Larkin', *London Magazine*, 1 (Feb 1962) 32.
19. Thom Gunn, 'Lines for a Book', *The Sense of Movement* (London: Faber and Faber, 1957) p. 30.
20. Larkin, in *Viewpoints*, p. 128.
21. Thwaite, 'The Poetry of Philip Larkin', in *The Survival of Poetry*, p. 48.
22. Larkin, in *Viewpoints*, p. 128.
23. Philip Larkin, 'The Puddletown Martyr', *New Statesman*, 18 Apr 1975, p. 514.
24. Philip Larkin, 'Wanted: Good Hardy Critic', *Critical Quarterly*, 8 (1966) 177–8.
25. A. E. Housman, letter to Katherine Symons, 5 Oct 1915, in *The Letters of A. E. Housman*, ed. Henry Maas (Cambridge, Mass.: Harvard University Press, 1971) p. 141.
26. Frederick Grubb, *A Vision of Reality: A Study of Liberalism in Twentieth Century Verse* (New York: Barnes and Noble, 1965) p. 229.
27. William Wordsworth, 'Lines Composed a Few Miles above Tintern Abbey' (1798) in *The Poetical Works of William Wordsworth*, ed. Ernest De Selincourt (London: Oxford University Press, 1965) p. 164.
28. Larkin, 'Betjeman En Bloc', *Listen*, 3, p. 15.
29. Larkin, in *Viewpoints*, p. 118.
30. D. W. Harding, 'Aspects of the Poetry of Isaac Rosenberg', *Scrutiny*, 3 (1934) 363–4.
31. Larkin, in *Viewpoints*, p. 116.

CHAPTER THREE: HUNGER OF THE IMAGINATION

1. For a discussion of Donald Davie's interests in this regard, see Blake Morrison, *The Movement* (Oxford: Oxford University Press, 1980), esp. pp. 37–9 and 109–10. Davie's *Purity of Diction in English Verse* (1952; repr. with

postscript, London: Routledge and Kegan Paul, 1967) is a valuable statement of his concerns as a Movement poet to revitalise contemporary poetry with the clarity and rigour of the Augustans. See particularly his chapter on Johnson's 'Vanity of Human Wishes' (pp. 82–90), and 'A Postscript, 1966' (pp. 197–202), wherein he says of the Movement writers, 'I like to think that if the group of us had ever cohered enough to subscribe to a common manifesto, it might have been *Purity of Diction in English Verse*' (p. 197).

2. See Petch, *The Art of Philip Larkin*. For other studies which relate Larkin's poetry to the concerns of the Augustans, see Bateson, 'Auden's (and Empson's) Heirs', *Essays in Criticism*, 7, pp. 76–80; and Alun R. Jones, 'The Poetry of Philip Larkin: A Note on Transatlantic Culture', *Western Humanities Review*, 16 (1962) 143–52.

3. Samuel Johnson, *The History of Rasselas, Prince of Abissinia* (1759), ed. with intro. Geoffrey Tillotson and Brian Jenkins (Oxford: Oxford University Press, 1977) pp. 85 and 114.

4. Richard Murphy, 'The Art of Debunkery', review of *High Windows*, in *New York Review of Books*, 15 May 1975, p. 30.

5. See Petch, *The Art of Philip Larkin*; and John Reibetanz, '*The Whitsun Weddings*: Larkin's Reinterpretation of Time and Form in Keats', *Contemporary Literature*, 17 (1976) 529–40.

6. Johnson, *The History of Rasselas*, p. 33.

7. Philip Larkin, *All What Jazz: A Record Diary 1961–68* (London: Faber and Faber, 1970) p. 17.

8. Northrop Frye, *The Modern Century* (Toronto: Oxford University Press, 1967), p. 61.

9. Donald Davie, quoted by Morrison in *The Movement*, p. 278.

10. D. J. Enright, *Literature for Man's Sake* (1955: repr. Tokyo: Norwood Editions, 1976) p. 189.

11. T. E. Hulme, 'Romanticism and Classicism' (1924) in *Prose Keys to Modern Poetry*, ed. Karl Shapiro (New York: Harper and Row, 1962) pp. 94–5; emphasis added.

12. Percy Bysshe Shelley, *Adonais* (1821), in *Selected Poetry and Prose of Shelley*, ed. Carlos Baker (New York: Charles Scribner's Sons, 1951) p. 306.

13. Hulme, 'Romanticism and Classicism', in *Prose Keys*, pp. 103–4.

14. Philip Larkin, in *Let the Poet Choose*, ed. James Gibson (London: Harrap, 1973). For another instance in which Larkin more recently uses this diction, see *Viewpoints*, p. 118. Moreover, Larkin employs his locution again in a recent *Paris Review* interview. When asked the central question, 'In your case, what is it you are preserving in your poems?', he replied, 'Well, as I said, the experience. The beauty.' See 'The Art of Poetry xxx: Philip Larkin', *Paris Review*, no. 84 (1982) 61.

15. For a series of other commentaries on Larkin's filiations with Keats and other Romantic figures, see Bibliography for items by John Bayley, Geoffrey Harvey and John Reibetanz. John Bayley, 'Larkin and the Romantic Tradition', *Critical Quarterly*, 26, nos 1–2 (Spring–Summer 1984) 61–6; Geoffrey Harvey, 'Creative Embarrassment: Philip Larkin's Dramatic Monologues', *Ariel: A Review of International English Literature*, 14, no. 1 (Jan 1983) 63–80; and John Reibetanz, '*The Whitsun Weddings*', *Contemporary*

Literature, 17, pp. 529–40, and 'Philip Larkin: The Particular Vision of *The Whitsun Weddings*', *Modern Language Quarterly*, 43, No. 2 (June 1982) 156–73.

CHAPTER FOUR: SOLITARY WONDER

1. Philip Larkin, 'Vernon Watkins: an Encounter and Re-encounter', in *Vernon Watkins: 1906–1967*, ed. Leslie Norris (London: Faber and Faber, 1970) p. 30. For other instances in which Larkin speaks of his esteem for Lawrence, see his 'Bertrand Russell and D. H. Lawrence', *Radio Times* 18 July 1952, p. 4, wherein he speaks of the 'vitality, humour, and penetration' of Lawrence; and *Viewpoints*, p. 120.
2. Larkin, 'Betjeman En Bloc', *Listen*, 3, p. 15.
3. Philip Larkin, 'Aubade', *Times Literary Supplement*, 23 Dec 1977, p. 1491.
4. *The Complete Poems of D. H. Lawrence*, ed. Vivian de Sola Pinto and Warren Roberts (New York: Viking Press, 1964) p. 525.
5. Ibid., p. 136.
6. At the risk of overstressing the point, I offer the following list of additional examples from Lawrence of poems which serve to indicate a mutuality in the poets' thematic and imagistic usages. All page references are to Lawrence's *Complete Poems*: 'From a College Window' (p. 35); 'Flat Suburbs, S. W., in the Morning' (p. 50); 'Suburbs on a Hazy Day' (p. 53); 'At the Window' (p. 102); 'New Heaven and Earth' (p. 256); 'Things Men Have Made' (p. 448); 'Escape' (p. 482); 'Beautiful Old Age' (p. 503); 'At Last' (p. 514); 'The Sane Universe' (p. 515); 'Young Fathers' (p. 521); 'Democracy' (p. 526); 'Desire' (p. 602); 'People' (p. 602); 'Loneliness' (p. 610); 'The Uprooted' (p. 610); 'Image-Making Love' (p. 610); 'What Have They Done to You' (p. 630); 'City-Life' (p. 632); 'False Democracy and Real' (p. 650); 'The Breath of Life' (p. 698); 'Man of the Sea' (p. 705); 'The End, the Beginning' (p. 724); 'Rebuked' (p. 731); 'Labour Battalion' (p. 746); 'The Elements' (p. 840); 'Deeper than Love' (p. 844); 'The Worm Turns' (p. 855).
7. Larkin, in *Viewpoints*, p. 127.
8. See Barbara Everett, 'Philip Larkin: After Symbolism', *Essays in Criticism*, 30 (1980) 227–42.
9. Lawrence, *Complete Poems*, p. 610.
10. For a study which relates Larkin's loneliness to Hardy's example, see Mary Ford, 'Loneliness Clarifies: A Study of the Longer Poems of Philip Larkin', *English Studies in Canada*, 7 (1980) 323–32.
11. Lawrence, *Complete Poems*, p. 610.
12. D. H. Lawrence, 'Morality and the Novel', in *D. H. Lawrence: Selected Literary Criticism*, ed. Anthony Beal (1956; repr. London: Heinemann, 1964) p. 109.
13. Ibid.
14. D. H. Lawrence, *Apocalypse* (1931), intro. Richard Aldington (London: Heinemann, 1972) p. 104.
15. D. H. Lawrence, 'Aristocracy', in *Phoenix II*, ed. with intro. Warren Roberts and Harry T. Moore (New York: Viking Press, 1968) pp. 481–2.

16. D. H. Lawrence, *The Rainbow* (1915; repr. Harmondsworth: Penguin Books, 1971) pp. 495–6.
17. Ibid., pp. 134–55.
18. Lawrence, *Complete Poems*, p. 73.
19. Johnson, *The History of Rasselas*, pp. 27–8.
20. Thomas Hardy, 'In Tenebris', in *Collected Poems of Thomas Hardy* (1930; repr. London: Macmillan, 1962) p. 154.

CHAPTER FIVE: FAMILY AND NATION

1. Larkin, in *Viewpoints*, p. 124.
2. Lawrence, *Apocalypse*, p. 104.
3. Lawrence, *The Rainbow*, pp. 133–4.
4. Larkin, in *Viewpoints*, pp. 124–5.
5. Lawrence, *Complete Poems*, pp. 162–3. See also, 'A Train at Night' (ibid., p. 861) and 'The Train' (ibid., p. 873).
6. Ibid., p. 673.
7. Philip Larkin, 'The Writer in his Age', *London Magazine*, 4, no. 5 (May 1957) 47.
8. Lawrence, *Selected Literary Criticism*, p. 109.
9. Philip Larkin, as quoted by Anthony Thwaite from a BBC broadcast. See Thwaite, 'The Poetry of Philip Larkin', in *The Survival of Poetry*, p. 51.
10. For those who might wish to pursue the historical significance of shifts in artistic approaches to reality, I would highly recommend the work of Owen Barfield, especially his *Saving the Appearances: A Study in Idolatry* (New York: Harcourt, Brace and World, 1965) chs 6 (pp. 40–5) and 11 (pp. 71–8). For a related study of the price of dislocation from reality in modern poetry, see R. K. Meiner's excellent essay, 'On Modern Poetry, Poetic Consciousness, and the Madness of Poets', in *Evolution of Consciousness: Studies in Polarity*, ed. Shirley Sugerman (Middletown Conn.: Wesleyan University Press, 1976) pp. 106–20.
11. Colin Falck, 'Cranking the Engine', review of *Imagist Poets*, in *Poetry Nation*, 1 (1973) 129. For an important study which deals with the value of the Imagist example in post-war American poetry, see Robert Pinsky, *The Situation of Poetry: Contemporary Poetry and its Traditions* (Princeton, NJ: Princeton University Press, 1976).
12. William Pratt, Introduction to *The Imagist Poem: Modern Poetry in Miniature* (New York: Dutton, 1963) p. 38.

CHAPTER SIX: POETRY OF REALITY

1. Larkin, *All What Jazz*, p. 17.
2. Larkin, in 'Four Conversations', *London Magazine*, 4, pp. 71–2.
3. Recent shifts in this tendency to see Larkin's work in the context of the

Modernists are visible in Barbara Everett's view of Larkin as a post-Symbolist poet and in both Andrew Motion's and Simon Petch's books on Larkin, wherein they stress Larkin's affinities with W. B. Yeats. For what I think is one of the best analyses of Larkin's Georgian affinities, see Edna Longley, 'Larkin, Edward Thomas and the Tradition', *Phoenix*, nos 11–12 (Fall–Winter 1973–4) 63–9.

4. Larkin, in 'The Art of Poetry xxx', *Paris Review*, no. 84, p. 67. As a measure of Larkin's care, on the issue, to separate what he admires from what he chooses not to, note his comment 'I admire *Murder in the Cathedral* as much as anything Eliot ever wrote. I read it from time to time, for pleasure, which is the highest compliment I can pay' (p. 59).

5. Robert Conquest, *New Lines* (1956; repr. New York: St Martin's Press, 1967) p. xv.

6. Wallace Stevens, 'Esthétique du Mal', in *The Collected Poems of Wallace Stevens* (New York: Alfred A. Knopf, 1957) p. 325.

7. Philip Larkin, 'Subsidies and Side Effects', *Times Literary Supplement*, 18 Feb 1977, p. 183.

8. Philip Larkin, 'The Poetry of William Barnes', review of *The Poems of William Barnes*, in *Listener*, 16 Aug 1962, p. 257.

9. Philip Larkin, 'What's Become of Wystan', review of *Homage to Clio*, in *Spectator*, 15 July 1960, p. 104.

10. Larkin, Introduction to Betjeman, *Collected Poems*, p. xxiii.

11. Larkin, 'Betjeman En Bloc', *Listen*, 3, p. 15.

12. Philip Larkin, 'The Blending of Betjeman', review of *Summoned By Bells* and *First and Last Loves*, in *Spectator*, 2 Dec 1960, p. 913.

13. Larkin, 'Larkin Praises the Poetry of Hardy', *Listener*, 25 July 1968, p. 111.

14. Ibid., p. 111.

15. Hardy comes closest to a statement of his own imagistic bias, I think, in his comment that 'Unadjusted impressions have their value, and the road to a true philosophy of life seems to lie in humbly recording diverse readings of its phenomena as they are forced upon us by chance and change.' See his Preface to *Poems of the Past and Present*, in *Collected Poems*, p. 75.

16. Hulme, 'Romanticism and Classicism', in *Prose Keys*, p. 101.

17. Ibid., p. 102.

18. Ibid., p. 101. Hulme's diction is very close to Larkin's claim, 'As a guiding principle I believe that every poem must be its own sole freshly created universe, and therefore have no belief in "tradition" or common myth-kitty . . .' – quoted by John Press in *A Map of Modern English Verse* (London: Oxford University Press, 1969) p. 258, from *Poets of the 1950's: An Anthology of New English Verse*, ed. D. J. Enright (Tokyo: Kenkyusha Press, 1955) pp. 77–8.

19. Randall Jarrell, 'An Introduction to the Selected Poems of William Carlos Williams' (1948) repr. in *Poetry and the Age* (New York: Vintage Books, 1955) p. 217.

20. Ezra Pound, 'A Few Don'ts' (1913), repr. in Shapiro, *Prose Keys*, p. 109.

21. Wallace Stevens, 'Imagination as Value' (1949), excerpted in *The Modern Tradition*, ed. Richard Ellmann and Charles Feidelson, Jr. (New York: Oxford University Press, 1965) p. 223.

22. Ibid., p. 222.

23. Wallace Stevens, 'Adagia', in *Opus Posthumous*, ed. with intro. Samuel French Morse (New York: Alfred A. Knopf, 1966) p. 162.
24. Philip Larkin, in *Poets of the 1950's*, pp. 77–8.
25. T. E. Hulme, 'Notes on Language and Style' (1925), repr. in *Further Speculations*, ed. Sam Hynes (Minneapolis: University of Minnesota Press, 1955) p. 99.
26. Pound, 'A Few Don'ts', in Shapiro, *Prose Keys*, p. 105.
27. Thwaite, 'The Poetry of Philip Larkin', in *The Survival of Poetry*, p. 43.
28. Ibid., p. 48. Thwaite tells us that Larkin once said to him that in the reading of 'The Whitsun Weddings', as the voice comes to the close, it should 'lift off the ground'.
29. Hulme, 'Romanticism and Classicism', in Shapiro, *Prose Keys*, p. 103.
30. Stevens, 'Adagia', *Opus Posthumous*, p. 173.
31. Wallace Stevens, *The Necessary Angel* (1951), excerpted in *The Modern Tradition*, p. 225.
32. Larkin, in *Viewpoints* p. 129.
33. Larkin, 'Four Conversations', *London Magazine*, 4, p. 73.

CHAPTER SEVEN: LARKIN'S PROPER PEERS

1. Thom Gunn, 'Modes of Control', *Yale Review*, 53 (1964) 447, 449 and 448. The phrase is quoted by Gunn from an untitled poem by Alan Stephens.
2. Thom Gunn, 'A Snow Vision', in *Poems 1950–1966: A Selection* (London: Faber and Faber, 1969) p. 43.
3. Stevens, 'Esthétique du Mal', in *Collected Poems*, p. 325.
4. Gunn, *The Sense of Movement*, p. 18.
5. Ted Hughes, *Poetry in the Making* (London: Faber and Faber, 1967) p. 18.
6. Ibid., pp. 18–19.
7. Ted Hughes, *Selected Poems: 1957–1967* (New York: Harper and Row, 1973) p. 3.
8. Ibid., p. 50.
9. Ibid., p. 35.
10. Ted Hughes, 'Crow Blacker than Ever', in *Crow* (New York: Harper and Row, 1971) p. 57.
11. Ibid., p. 9.
12. *Macbeth*, iii.ii.50–1, cited from *William Shakespeare: The Complete Works*, ed. Alfred Harbage (Baltimore: Penguin Books, 1969) p. 1122.
13. Hughes, *Poetry in the Making*, p. 43.
14. Hughes, *Selected Poems*, p. 13.
15. Hughes, *Poetry in the Making*, p. 34.
16. Ibid., p. 76.
17. Ibid., p. 124.
18. Patrick Swinden, 'Thom Gunn's Castle', review of *Jack Straw's Castle*, in *Critical Quarterly*, 19 (1977) 43.
19. Gunn, in 'Four Conversations', *London Magazine*, 4, p. 69.
20. Ibid., p. 65.

21. Gunn, 'Modes of Control', *Yale Review*, 53, p. 448.
22. Thom Gunn, *Moly* (London: Faber and Faber, 1971) p. 14.
23. Ibid., p. 53.
24. Gunn, *Poems 1950–1966*, p. 28.
25. Derwent May, 'Burdens', review of *Jack Straw's Castle*, in *Listener*, 25 Nov 1976, p. 686.
26. Thom Gunn, *Jack Straw's Castle* (London: Faber and Faber, 1976) p. 14.
27. Ibid., p. 15.
28. Ibid., p. 27.
29. Ibid., p. 22.
30. Ibid.
31. Gunn, *Poems 1950–1966*, p. 43.
32. John Press, *Rule and Energy: Trends in British Poetry Since the Second World War* (London: Oxford University Press, 1963) p. 149.
33. Ibid., p. 140.
34. R. S. Thomas, *Poetry for Supper* (London: Rupert Hart-Davis, 1967) p. 34.
35. R. S. Thomas, 'A Peasant', in *The New Poetry* ed. with intro. A. Alvarez (Harmondsworth: Penguin Books, 1962) p. 77.
36. Thomas, *Poetry for Supper*, p. 20.
37. R. S. Thomas, *Pietà* (London: Rupert Hart-Davis, 1966) p. 44.
38. R. S. Thomas, *H'm* (London: Macmillan, 1972) p. 17.
39. Ibid., p. 16.
40. Ibid., p. 30.
41. R. S. Thomas, *Later Poems: 1972–1982* (London: Macmillan, 1983) pp. 66–7.
42. Ibid., p. 155.
43. Ibid., p. 103.
44. Ibid., p. 117.
45. Enright, *Literature for Man's Sake*, pp. 203–4.

Bibliography

PRIMARY

English Romantic Poetry and Prose, ed. Noyes Russell (New York: Oxford University Press, 1956).

Gunn, Thom, 'Four Conversations', interview with Ian Hamilton, *London Magazine*, 4 (Nov 1964) 64–70.

——, *Jack Straw's Castle* (London: Faber and Faber, 1976).

——, 'Modes of Control', *Yale Review*, 53 (1964) 447–58.

——, *Moly* (London: Faber and Faber, 1971).

——, *Poems 1950–1966: A Selection* (London: Faber and Faber, 1969).

——, *The Sense of Movement* (London: Faber and Faber, 1957).

Hardy, Thomas, *The Collected Poems of Thomas Hardy* (London: Macmillan, 1962).

Housman, A. E., *The Letters of A. E. Housman*, ed. Henry Maas (Cambridge, Mass.: Harvard University Press, 1971).

Hughes, Ted, *Crow* (New York: Harper and Row, 1971).

——, *Poetry in the Making* (London: Faber and Faber, 1967).

——, *Selected Poems: 1957–1967* (New York: Harper and Row, 1973).

Hughes, Ted, and Godwin, Fay, *Remains of Elmet: A Pennine Sequence*, poems by Ted Hughes, photographs by Fay Godwin (London and Boston, Mass.: Faber and Faber, 1979).

Hughes, Ted, and Gunn, Thom, *Selected Poems* (London: Faber and Faber, 1962).

Hughes, Ted, and Keen, Peter, *River*, poems by Ted Hughes, photographs by Peter Keen (London and Boston, Mass.: Faber and Faber, in association with James and James, 1983).

Hughes, Ted, and Thomas, R. S., *Ted Hughes and R. S. Thomas Read and Discuss Selections of their Own Poems*, audio tape in the Critical Forum series (Battle, Sussex: Norwich Tapes, 1978).

Hulme, T. E., *Further Speculations*, ed. Sam Hynes (Minneapolis: University of Minnesota Press, 1955).

——, 'Romanticism and Classicism' (1924), repr. in *Prose Keys to Modern Poetry*, ed. Karl Shapiro (New York: Harper and Row, 1962).

——, *Speculations: Essays on Humanism and the Philosophy of Art*, 2nd edn (1924; repr. London: Kegan Paul, Trench and Trübner, 1936).

The Imagist Poem: Modern Poetry in Miniature, ed. with intro. William Pratt (New York: Dutton, 1963).

Imagist Poetry, ed. with intro. Peter Jones (Harmondsworth: Penguin, 1972).

Johnson, Samuel, *The History of Rasselas, Prince of Abissinia* (1759) ed. with intro. Geoffrey Tillotson and Brian Jenkins (Oxford: Oxford University Press, 1977).

Larkin, Philip, *All What Jazz: A Record Diary 1961–68* (London: Faber and Faber, 1970).

——, 'Amis and Auden: Philip Larkin Compares Kingsley Amis' *New Oxford Book of Light Verse* with Auden's 1938 Selection', *New Review*, 5, no. 1 (1978) 92–4.

——, 'The Apollo Bit', review of *The Letters of Rupert Brooke*, ed. Sir Geoffrey Keynes, in *New Statesman*, 14 June 1968, pp. 798–802.

——, 'The Art of Poetry xxx: Philip Larkin', interview with Robert Phillips, *Paris Review*, no. 84 (1982) 42–72.

——, 'Aubade', *Times Literary Supplement*, 23 Dec 1977, p. 1491.

——, 'W. H. Auden (1907–1973)', short tributes to W. H. Auden's memory by various contemporary poets and critics, in *New Statesman*, 5 Oct 1973, p. 479.

——, 'The Batman from Blades', review of John Gardner, *Licence Renewed*, *Times Literary Supplement*, 5 June 1981, p. 625.

——, 'Betjeman En Bloc', review of John Betjeman, *Collected Poems*, *Listen*, 3 (Spring 1959) 14–22.

——, 'Big Victims: Emily Dickinson and Walter de la Mare', review of *The Complete Poems of Emily Dickinson*, ed. Thomas H. Johnson, and *The Complete Poems of Walter de la Mare*, in *New Statesman*, 13 Mar 1970, pp. 367–8.

——, 'The Blending of Betjeman', review of John Betjeman, *Summoned by Bells* and *First and Last Loves*, in *Spectator*, 2 Dec 1960, p. 913.

——, 'Bertrand Russell and D. H. Lawrence', letter in *Radio Times*, 18 July 1952, p. 4.

——, 'Breadfruit', *Critical Quarterly*, 3 (1961) 309.

——, comment on 'Absences', in *Poet's Choice*, ed. Paul Engle and Joseph Langland (New York: Dial Press, 1962) p. 202.

——, comment on 'MCMXIV' and 'Send No Money', in *Let the Poet Choose*, ed. James Gibson (London: Harrap, 1973) p. 102.

——, 'Context: Philip Larkin', *London Magazine*, 1 (Feb 1962) 31–2.

——, 'Four Conversations', interview with Ian Hamilton, *London Magazine*, 4 (Nov 1964) 71–7.

——, 'Frivolous and Vulnerable', *New Statesman*, 28 Sep 1962, pp. 416–18.

——, *A Girl in Winter* (1947; repr. London: Faber and Faber, 1964).

——, 'The Hidden Hardy', review of *One Rare Fair Woman: Hardy's Letters to Florence Henniker, 1893–1922*, ed. Evelyn Hardy and F. B. Pinion, in *New Statesman*, 2 June 1972, pp. 752–3.

——, *High Windows* (London: Faber and Faber, 1974).

——, Introduction to John Betjeman, *Collected Poems*, compiled by the Earl of Birkenhead (Boston Mass.: Houghton Mifflin, 1971) pp. xvii–xli.

——, 'In the Seventies', review of *The Collected Letters of Thomas Hardy*, vol. I: *1840–1892*, ed. Richard Little Purdy and Michael Millgate, in *New Statesman*, 27 Jan 1978, pp. 116–17.

——, *Jill* (1946; repr. London: Faber and Faber, 1957).

——, 'Larkinland', comment on a reading of his poetry, *Listener*, 4 Aug 1977, p. 143.

——, *The Less Deceived* (1955; repr. Hessle: Marvell Press, 1966).

——, 'The Life with a Hole in It', in *Poetry Supplement* for the Poetry Book Society, compiled by Philip Larkin (London: Poetry Book Society, 1974).

——, 'Love', *Critical Quarterly*, 8 (1966) 173.

——, 'Master's Voices', review of Francis Berry's *Poetry and the Physical Voice*, Donald Dawe's *A Sequence for Francis Parkman*, and poetry readings recorded by John Betjeman, Louis MacNeice and Dylan Thomas, in *New Statesman*, 2 Feb 1962, pp. 169–70.

——, 'The Most Victorian Laureate', review of *The Poems of Tennyson*, ed. Christopher Ricks, in *New Statesman*, 14 Mar 1969, pp. 363–4.

——, 'Mr Powell's Mural', review of Anthony Powell, *Books Do Furnish a Room*, in *New Statesman*, 19 Feb 1971, pp. 243–4.

——, 'Mrs Hardy's Memories', review of *Young Hardy: Some Recollections*, ed. Evelyn Hardy and Robert Gittings, together with some relevant poems by Thomas Hardy, in *Critical Quarterly*, 4 (1962) 75–9.

——, 'A Neglected Responsibility: Contemporary Literary Manuscripts', *Encounter*, 53 (July 1979) 33–41.

——, *The North Ship* (1945; repr. with intro., London: Faber and Faber, 1966).

——, 'Out of the Air: Not Like Larkin', comment on the occasion of his fiftieth birthday, *Listener*, 17 Aug 1972, p. 209.

——, 'The Pleasure Principle', review of Vernon Scannell's *A Mortal Pitch*, Christopher Logue's *Devil, Maggot, and Son*, and John Press's *Uncertainties, and Other Poems*, in *Listen*, 2 (Summer–Autumn 1957) 28–32.

——, 'The Poetry of William Barnes', review of *The Poems of William Barnes*, ed. Bernard Jones, *Listener*, 16 Aug 1962, p. 257.

——, 'Philip Larkin Praises the Poetry of Thomas Hardy', *Listener*, 25 July 1968, p. 111.

——, *Philip Larkin, 'High Windows': Poems Read by the Author*, recording, Argo Records, ed. Peter Orr, with a commentary by Charles Osborne on sleeve (London: Argo, 1974; Decca Records, 1975).

——, *Philip Larkin Reads and Comments on 'The Whitsun Weddings'*, recording, Listen Records, ed. George Hartley, with a review of *The Whitsun Weddings* by Christopher Ricks (repr. from 'A True Poet', *New York Review of Books*, 28 Jan 1965, pp. 10–11) on sleeve (London: Listen Records, 1965; Hessle: Marvell Press, 1965).

——, *Philip Larkin Reads 'The Less Deceived'*, recording, Listen Records, ed. George Hartley, and an interview with Larkin by Hartley on sleeve (London: Listen Records, 1958; Hessle: Marvell Press, 1968).

——, 'The Puddletown Martyr', review of Robert Gittings, *Young Thomas Hardy*, in *New Statesman*, 18 Apr 1975, pp. 514–15.

——, 'The Real Wilfred: Owen's Life and Legends', review of Jon Stallworthy, *Wilfred Owen*, in *Encounter*, 44 (May 1975) 73–81.

——, *Required Writing: Miscellaneous Pieces 1955–1982* (London and Boston, Mass.: Faber and Faber, 1983).

——, review of Lona Mosk Packer, *Christina Rossetti*, and *The Rossetti–Macmillan Letters*, ed. Lona Mosk Packer, in *Listener*, 26 Mar 1964, p. 526.

——, review of John Press, *Guy Fawkes, and Other Poems*, in *Critical Quarterly*, 1 (1959) 362–3.

——, 'Superlatively Alone', review of George Eells, *The Life that Lately he Led: A Biography of Cole Porter*, in *Guardian*, 18 Aug 1967, p. 5.

——, 'Shelving the Issue', review of Thomas and Edith Kelly, *Books for the People: An Illustrated History of the British Public Library*, in *New Statesman*, 10 June 1977, pp. 783–4.

——, 'The State of Poetry – A Symposium', *Review*, nos 29–30 (Spring–Summer 1972) p. 60.

——, 'Subsidies and Side Effects', speech on the occasion of accepting the Shakespeare Prize, *Times Literary Supplement*, 18 Feb 1977, p. 183.

——, 'Things Noticed', review of *The Personal Notebooks of Thomas Hardy*, ed. Richard H. Taylor, in *New Statesman*, 4 May 1979, pp. 642–3.

——, in *Viewpoints: Poets in Conversation*, interviews collected by John Haffenden with preface (London: Faber and Faber, 1981).

——, 'Vernon Watkins: An Encounter and a Re-encounter', in *Vernon Watkins: 1906–1967*, ed. Leslie Norris (London: Faber and Faber, 1970) pp. 28–34.

——, 'Wanted: Good Hardy Critic', review of Roy Morrell, *Thomas Hardy: The Will and the Way*, in *Critical Quarterly*, 8 (1966) 174–9.

——, 'The War Poet', review of *The Collected Poems of Wilfred Owen*, ed. C. Day Lewis, *Listener*, 10 Oct 1963, pp. 561–2.

——, 'What's Become of Wystan?', review of W. H. Auden, *Homage to Clio*, in *Spectator*, 15 July 1960, pp. 104–5.

——, *The Whitsun Weddings* (London: Faber and Faber, 1964).

——, 'Words for Music, Perhaps', review of Donald Mitchell, *Britten and Auden in the Thirties: The Year 1936*, in *Times Literary Supplement*, 27 Feb 1981, p. 222.

——, 'The World of Barbara Pym', *Times Literary Supplement*, 11 Mar 1977, p. 260.

——, 'The Writer in his Age: Philip Larkin', *London Magazine*, 4 (May 1957) pp. 46–7.

Lawrence, D. H., *Apocalypse* (1931), intro. Richard Aldington (London: Heinemann, 1972).

——, 'Christ's in Tirol', in *The Portable D. H. Lawrence*, ed. with intro. Diana Trilling (New York: Viking Press, 1946).

——, *The Complete Poems of D. H. Lawrence*, ed. Vivian de Sola Pinto and Warren Roberts (New York: Viking Press, 1964).

——, *Phoenix II: Uncollected, Unpublished, and Other Prose Works by D. H. Lawrence*, collected and ed. with notes and intro. Warren Roberts and Harry T. Moore (New York: Viking Press, 1968).

——, *The Rainbow* (1915; repr. Harmondsworth; Penguin Books, 1971).

——, *Selected Literary Criticism*, ed. with intro. Anthony Beal (1956; repr. London: Heinemann, 1964).

The Modern Tradition: Backgrounds of Modern Literature, ed. Richard Ellmann and Charles Feidelson, Jr (New York: Oxford University Press, 1965).

New Lines, ed. with intro. Robert Conquest (1956; repr. New York: St Martin's Press, 1967).

New Lines II, ed. with intro. Robert Conquest (London: Macmillan, 1963).

The New Poetry, ed. A. Alvarez (1962; repr. Harmondsworth: Penguin, 1967).

The Oxford Book of Twentieth-Century English Verse, ed. Philip Larkin (Oxford: Clarendon Press, 1973).

The Penguin Book of Contemporary British Poetry, ed. Blake Morrison and Andrew Motion (Harmondsworth: Penguin, 1982).

The Penguin Book of Contemporary Verse: 1918–1960, ed. with intro. Kenneth Allott (1950; repr. with revisions, Harmondsworth: Penguin, 1965).

Poets of the 1950's: An Anthology of New English Verse, ed. D. J. Enright (Tokyo: Kenkyusha Press, 1955).

Pound, Ezra, 'A Few Don'ts' (1913), repr. in *Prose Keys to Modern Poetry*, ed. Karl Shapiro (New York: Harper and Row, 1962).
——, 'Vorticism', *Fortnightly Review*, 96 (1914) 461–71.
Shakespeare, William, *The Complete Works*, ed. Alfred Harbage (Baltimore: Penguin Books, 1969).
Shelley, Percy Bysshe, *Selected Poetry and Prose of Shelley*, ed. Carlos Baker (New York: Charles Scribner's Sons, 1951).
Stevens, Wallace, *The Collected Poems of Wallace Stevens* (New York: Alfred A. Knopf, 1957).
——, 'Imagination as Value' (1949) excerpted in *The Modern Tradition*, ed. Richard Ellmann and Charles Feidelson, Jr (New York: Oxford University Press, 1965).
——, *The Necessary Angel* (1951), excerpted ibid.
——, *Opus Posthumous* (1957), ed. with intro. Samuel French Morse (New York: Alfred A. Knopf, 1966).
Thomas, R. S., *Frequencies* (London: Macmillan, 1978).
——, *H'm* (London: Macmillan, 1972).
——, *R. S. Thomas: Later Poems 1972–1982* (London: Macmillan, 1983).
——, *Pietà* (London: Rupert Hart-Davis, 1966).
——, *Poetry for Supper* (London: Rupert Hart-Davis, 1967).
Wordsworth, William, *The Poetical Works of William Wordsworth*, ed. Ernest De Selincourt (London: Oxford University Press, 1965).

SECONDARY

Alvarez, A., *Beyond All This Fiddle: Essays 1955–1967* (New York: Random House, 1968).
——, *The Savage God: A Study of Suicide* (1971; repr. Harmondsworth: Penguin Books, 1974).
Anon., review of *High Windows*, in *Virginia Quarterly Review*, 52 (1976) 50.
——, 'In the Movement', *Spectator*, 1 Oct 1954, 399–400.
——, 'Poetic Moods', review of *The Less Deceived*, in *Times Literary Supplement*, 16 Dec 1955, p. 762.
——, 'Undeceived Poet', review of *The Whitsun Weddings*, in *Times Literary Supplement*, 12 Mar 1964, p. 216.
Ball, Patricia, 'The Photographic Art', *Review of English Literature*, 3 (1962) 50–8.
Barfield, Owen, *Saving the Appearances: A Study in Idolatry* (New York: Harcourt, Brace and World, 1965).
Bateson, F. W., 'Auden's (and Empson's) Heirs', review of *The Less Deceived* and Donald Davie's *Brides of Reason*, in *Essays in Criticism*, 7 (1957) 76–80.
Bayley, John, 'Too Good for This World', review of *High Windows*, in *Times Literary Supplement*, 21 June 1974, pp. 653–5.
——, 'Inside Out', review of Gavin Ewart, *The Collected Ewart 1933–1980*, and Michael Cook, *Selected Poems and Prose*, in *London Review of Books*, 2, no. 17 (Sep 1980) 22–3.
——, 'Larkin and the Romantic Tradition', *Critical Quarterly*, 26, nos 1–2 (Spring–Summer 1984) 61–6.

Bedient, Calvin, *Eight Contemporary Poets* (London: Oxford University Press, 1974).

——, 'On Ted Hughes', *Critical Quarterly*, 14 (1972) 103–24.

Bergonzi, Bernard, 'After "The Movement"', *Listener*, 24 Aug 1961, pp. 283–6.

——, 'Davie, Larkin, and the State of England', *Contemporary Literature*, 18 (Summer 1977) 343–60.

Betjeman, John, 'Common Experiences', review of *The Whitsun Weddings*, in *Listener*, 19 Mar 1964, p. 483.

Blackburn, Thomas, *The Price of an Eye* (1961; repr. Westport, Conn: Greenwood Press, 1974).

Bloomfield, B. C., *Philip Larkin: A Bibliography, 1933–1976* (London: Faber and Faber, 1979).

Blum, Margaret, 'Larkin's "Dry-Point"', *Explicator*, 32 (1974) 48–9.

Bold, Alan, *Thom Gunn and Ted Hughes* (Edinburgh: Oliver and Boyd, 1976).

Bowen, Roger, 'Death, Failure, and Survival in the Poetry of Philip Larkin', *Dalhousie Review*, 58 (1978) 79–84.

——, 'Poet in Transition: Larkin's *XX Poems*', *Iowa Review*, 8 (1977) 87–104.

Brown, Merle, 'Larkin and his Audience', *Iowa Review*, 8 (1977) 117–34.

Brownjohn Alan, 'The Deep Blue Air', review of *High Windows*, in *New Statesman*, 14 June 1974, 855–6.

——, 'English Poetry in the Early Seventies', in *British Poetry Since 1960: A Critical Survey*, ed. Michael Schmidt and Grevel Lindop (Oxford: Carcanet Press, 1972).

——, *Philip Larkin*, Writers and their Work (London: Longman, for the British Council, 1975).

Coulette, Henri, 'The Thought of *High Windows*', review of *High Windows*, in *Southern Review*, 12 (1976) 438–41.

Cox, C. B., 'Philip Larkin, Anti-Heroic Poet', *Studies in the Literary Imagination*, 9 (1976) 155–68.

Craig, Cairns, 'Two Conservatisms of English Poetry', *Stand*, 20 (1977) 12–20.

Crispin, Edmund, 'An Oxford Group', review of *Jill*, in *Spectator*, 17 Apr 1964, p. 525.

Cushman, Keith, 'Larkin's Landscapes', *Modern British Literature*, 4 (1979) 109–19.

Daiches, David, review of *The Oxford Book of Twentieth-Century Verse*, in *Review of English Studies*, 24 (1973) 518–22.

Davie, Donald, *Ezra Pound: Poet as Sculptor* (New York: Oxford University Press, 1964).

——, *Pound* (London and Glasgow: Collins, 1975).

——, *Purity of Diction in English Verse* (1952; repr. London: Routledge and Kegan Paul, 1969).

——, *Thomas Hardy and British Poetry* (New York: Oxford University Press, 1972).

Davies, Walford, 'An Ordinary Sorrow of Man's Life', *Sewanee Review*, 74 (1976) 523–7.

Davison, Peter, 'The Gilt Edge of Reputation: Twelve Months of New Poetry', *Atlantic Monthly*, Jan 1966, pp. 82–5.

Dodsworth, Martin, 'The Climate of Pain in Recent Poetry', *London Magazine*, 4 (1964) 86–95.

Elon, Florence, 'The Movement against Itself: British Poetry of the 1950s', *Southern Review*, 19, no. 1 (Jan 1983) 88–110.

Enright, D. J., 'Down Cemetery Road', review of *The Whitsun Weddings* (1964), repr. in *Conspirators and Poets* (Chester Springs, Pa.: Dufour Editions, 1966).

——, *Literature for Man's Sake* (1955; repr. Tokyo: Norwood Editions, 1976).

Everett, Barbara, 'Philip Larkin: After Symbolism', *Essays in Criticism*, 30 (1980) 227–42.

——, 'Larkin's Edens', *English*, 31, no. 138 (Spring 1982) 41–53.

Falck, Colin, 'Cranking the Engine', review of *Imagist Poetry*, ed. Peter Jones, in *Poetry Nation*, no. 1 (1973) 126–9.

——, review of *The Whitsun Weddings*, in *Review*, 15 (Dec 1964) 3–11.

——, 'Think it Over', review of R. S. Thomas, *Frequencies*, in *New Review*, 5, no. 2 (1978) 120–4.

Ferguson, Peter, 'Philip Larkin's XX Poems: The Missing Link', *Agenda*, 14 (Autumn 1976) 53–65.

Ford, Mary, 'Loneliness Clarifies: A Study of the Longer Poems of Philip Larkin', *English Studies in Canada*, 7 (1980) 323–32.

Fraser, G. S., *The Modern Writer and his World: Continuity and Innovation in Twentieth-Century English Literature* (1953; repr. New York: Frederick A. Praeger, 1965).

——, 'Philip Larkin: the Lyric Note and the Grand Style', in *Essays On Twentieth-Century Poets* (Leicester: Leicester University Press, 1977) pp. 243–53.

——, *Vision and Rhetoric: Studies in Modern Poetry* (London: Faber and Faber, 1959).

Frye, Northrop, *The Modern Century: The Whidden Lectures, 1967* (Toronto: Oxford University Press, 1967).

Fuller, John, 'A Liking for Larkin', review of Lolette Kuby, *An Uncommon Poet for the Common Man*, in *Times Literary Supplement*, 24 Oct 1975, p. 1259.

Gardner, Philip, 'Bearing the Unbearable', review of *High Windows*, in *Phoenix*, no. 13 (Spring 1975) 94–100.

——, 'The Wintry Drum: The Poetry of Philip Larkin', *Dalhousie Review*, 48 (Winter 1968–9) 88–95.

Garfitt, Roger, 'In Retreat to the Edges', review of *High Windows*, in *London Magazine*, 14 (Oct–Nov 1974) 111–20.

Grubb, Frederick, 'Dragons', *Phoenix*, nos 11–12 (Autumn–Winter 1973–4) 119–36.

——, *A Vision of Reality: A Study of Liberalism in Twentieth Century Verse* (New York: Barnes and Noble, 1965).

Hahn, Claire, '*Crow* and the Biblical Creation Narratives', *Critical Quarterly*, 19 (1977) 43–54.

Hainsworth, J. D., 'A Poet of our Time', *Hibbert Journal*, 64 (1966) 153–5.

Hamilton, Ian, 'The Making of the Movement', in *British Poetry since 1960: A Critical Survey*, ed. Michael Schmidt and Grevel Lindop (Oxford: Carcanet Press, 1972) pp. 70–3.

——, *A Poetry Chronicle: Essays and Reviews*, (New York: Harper and Row, 1973).

Hamburger, Michael, *The Truth of Poetry: Tensions in Modern Poetry from Baudelaire to the 1960s* (London: Weidenfeld and Nicolson, 1969).

Harding, D. W., 'Aspects of the Poetry of Isaac Rosenberg', *Scrutiny*, 3 (1934) 380–97.

Harmer, J. B., *Victory in Limbo: Imagism 1908–1917* (London: Secker and Warburg, 1975).

Hartley, George, 'The Lost Displays', review of *High Windows*, in *Phoenix*, no. 13 (Spring 1975) 87–92.

——, 'No Right of Entry', *Phoenix*, nos 11–12 (Autumn–Winter 1973–4) 105–9.

Harvey, Geoffrey, 'Creative Embarrassment: Philip Larkin's Dramatic Monologues', *Ariel: A Review of International English Literature*, 14, no. 1. (Jan 1983) 63–80.

Heaney, Seamus, 'Now and in England', *Critical Inquiry*, 3 (1977) 471–89.

Hilliard, Stephen S., 'Wit and Beauty', review of *High Windows*, in *Prairie Schooner*, 49 (1975) 270–1.

Hirschberg, Herbert, 'Larkin's "Dry-Point": Life without Illusion', *Notes on Contemporary Literature*, 8, no. 1 (Jan 1978) 5–6.

Homberger, Eric, *The Art of the Real: Poetry in England and America since 1939* (London: J. M. Dent, 1977).

Hope, Francis, 'Philip Larkin', review of *The Whitsun Weddings* and *Jill*, in *Encounter*, 22 (May 1964) 72–4.

Hughes, Glenn, *Imagism and the Imagists: A Study in Modern Poetry* (1931; repr. New York: Biblo and Tannen, 1972).

Hynes, Samuel, 'The Hardy Tradition in Modern English Poetry', *Sewanee Review*, 88 (Winter 1980) 33–51.

Jacobson, Dan, 'Profile 3: Philip Larkin', *New Review*, 1 (June 1974) 25–9.

James, Clive, 'Wolves of Memory', review of *High Windows*, in *Encounter*, 42 (June 1974) 65–71.

Jarrell, Randall, *Poetry and the Age* (New York: Vintage Books, 1955).

Jennings, Elizabeth, 'The Larkin Tone', review of *The North Ship*, in *Spectator*, 23 Sep 1966, pp. 385–6.

Jones, Alun R., 'The Poetry of Philip Larkin: A Note on Transatlantic Culture', *Western Humanities Review*, 16 (1962) 143–52.

Kermode, Frank, 'Remembering the Movement, and Researching It', review of Blake Morrison *The Movement*, and *The Oxford Book of Contemporary Verse 1945–1980*, ed. D. J. Enright, in *London Review of Books*, 2, no. 11 (June 1989) 6–7.

King, P. R., *Nine Contemporary Poets: A Critical Introduction* (London and New York: Methuen, 1979).

Kuby, Lolette, *An Uncommon Poet for the Common Man: A Study of Philip Larkin's Poetry* (The Hague and Paris: Mouton, 1974).

The Language of Images, ed. W. J. T. Mitchell (Chicago and London: Chicago University Press, 1980).

Larkin at Sixty, ed. Anthony Thwaite (London: Faber and Faber, 1982).

Lavine, Steven David, 'Larkin's Supreme Versions', *Michigan Quarterly Review*, 15 (1976) 481–6.

Longley, Edna, 'Larkin, Edward Thomas and the Tradition', *Phoenix*, nos 11–12 (Fall–Winter 1973–74) 63–9.

Lowell, Robert, 'Digressions from Larkin's Twentieth-Century Verse', *Encounter*, 40 (May 1973) 66–8.

McLuhan, Marshall, *The Mechanical Bride: Folklore of Industrial Man* (New York: Vanguard Press, 1951).

MacSweeney, Kerry, 'That it Can't Come Again', review of *High Windows*, in *Queen's Quarterly*, 82 (1975) 317–20.

Martin, Bruce, *Philip Larkin*, Twayne's English Authors.no. 234, gen. ed. Kinley Roby (Boston, Mass.: G. K. Hall, 1978).

——, 'Philip Larkin', in *Dictionary of Literary Biography*, ed. Vincent B. Sherry, vol. xxvii: *Poets of Great Britain and Ireland 1945–1960* (Detroit: Gale Research, 1984) pp. 194–205.

May, Derwent, 'Burdens', review of Thom Gunn, of *Jack Straw's Castle*, in *Listener*, 25 Nov 1976, pp. 686–7.

Merchant, W. Moelwynn, *R. S. Thomas*, Writers of Wales, ed. Meic Stephens and R. Brinley Jones (n.p.: Univ. of Wales Press, on behalf of the Welsh Arts Council, 1979).

Meiner, R. K., 'On Modern Poetry, Poetic Consciousness, and the Madness of the Poets', in *Evolution of Consciousness: Studies in Polarity*, ed. Shirley Sugarman (Middletown, Conn.: Wesleyan University Press, 1976) pp. 106–20.

Milligan, Ian, 'Philip Larkin's "The Whitsun Weddings" and Virginia Woolf's *The Waves*', *Notes and Queries*, 23 (1976) 23.

Milosz, Czeslaw, 'The Real and the Paradigms', *Poetry Australia*, no. 72 (Oct 1979) 59–63.

The Modern Poet: Essays from 'The Review', ed. Ian Hamilton (London: Macdonald, 1968).

Modern Poetics, ed. James Scully (New York: McGraw-Hill, 1965).

Moon, Kenneth, 'Cosmic Perspective: A Use of Imagery in the Poetry of Philip Larkin', *Poetry Australia*, no. 68 (Oct 1978) 59–63.

Morrison, Blake, *The Movement: English Poetry and Fiction of the 1950's* (Oxford: Oxford University Press, 1980).

——, 'The Movement: A Re-assessment (Part One)', *PN Review*, 4, no. 1 (1977) 26–9, and '(Part Two)', *PN Review*, 4, no. 2 (1977) 43–8.

Motion, Andrew, *Philip Larkin*, Contemporary Writers, gen. eds Malcolm Bradbury and Christopher Bigsby (London and New York: Methuen, 1982).

Murphy, Richard, 'The Art of Debunkery', review of *High Windows*, in *New York Review of Books*, 15 May 1975, pp. 30–2.

Naremore, James, 'Philip Larkin's "Lost World" ', *Contemporary Literature*, 15 (1974) 331–44.

Newton, J. M., '. . . And a More Comprehensive Soul', review of *The Whitsun Weddings*, in *Cambridge Querterly*, 1 (1965) 96–101.

Nimmo, David C., review of *High Windows*, in *Dalhousie Review*, 55 (1975) 383–5.

Oates, Joyce Carol, review of *A Girl in Winter*, in *New Republic*, 20 Nov 1976, pp. 38–40.

Oakes, Philip, review of *Larkin at Sixty*, ed. Anthony Thwaite, in *Sunday Times*, 23 May 1982.

Oberg, Arthur, 'Larkin's Lark Eggs: The Vision is Sentimental', *Stand*, 18 (1976) 21–6.

O'Connor, William Van, *The New University Wits and thue End of Modernism* (Carbondale: Southern Illinois University Press, 1963).

Parkinson, R. N., 'To Keep Our Metaphysics Warm: A Study of "Church Going" by Philip Larkin', *Critical Survey*, 5 (1971) 224–33.

Perloff, Marjorie, 'The Two Poetries: An Introduction', *Contemporary Literature*, 18 (Summer 1977) 263–78.

Peschmann, Herman, 'Philip Larkin: Laureate of the Common Man', *English*, 24 (Summer 1975) 49–59.

Petch, Simon, *The Art of Philip Larkin*, Sydney Studies in Literature (Sydney: Sydney University Press, 1981).

Pinsky, Robert, *The Situation of Poetry: Contemporary Poetry and its Traditions* (Princeton: Princeton University Press, 1976).

Powell, Neill, *Carpenters of Light: Some Contemporary English Poets* (Manchester: Carcanet New Press, 1979).

Press, John, *A Map of Modern English Verse* (London: Oxford University Press, 1968).

——, 'The Poetry of Philip Larkin', *Southern Review*, 13 (1977) 131–46.

——, *Rule and Energy: Trends in British Poetry Since the Second World War* (London: Oxford University Press, 1963).

Pritchard, William H., 'Larkin Lives', review of *High Windows*, in *Hudson Review*, 27 (1975) 302–8.

Reibetanz, John, '*The Whitsun Weddings*: Larkin's Reinterpretation of Time and Form in Keats', *Contemporary Literature*, 17 (1976) 529–40.

——, 'Philip Larkin: The Particular Vision of *The Whitsun Weddings*', *Modern Language Quarterly*, 43, no. 2 (June 1982) 156–73.

Ricks, Christopher, 'A True Poet', review of *The Whitsun Weddings*, in *New York Review of Books*, 28 Jan 1965, pp. 10–11.

Rosenthal, M. L., *The Modern Poets: A Critical Introduction* (1960; repr. London: Galaxy Books, 1965).

——, *The New Poets: American and British Poetry since World War II* (1967; repr. New York: Oxford University Press, 1968).

——, 'Tuning in on Albion', *Nation*, 16 May 1959, pp. 457–9.

——, and Gall, Sally M., 'The Modern Sequence and its Precursors', *Contemporary Literature*, 22 (Summer 1981) 308–25.

Sagar, Keith, *The Art of D. H. Lawrence* (Cambridge: Cambridge University Press, 1966).

——, *The Art of Ted Hughes* (Cambridge: Cambridge Univerity Press, 1975).

Scofield, Martin, 'The Poetry of Philip Larkin', *Massachusetts Review*, 17 (1976) 370–89.

Scupham, Peter, 'A Caucus-race', review of *The Oxford Book of Twentieth-Century English Verse*, in *Phoenix*, nos 11–12 (Autumn–Winter 1973–4) 173–82.

Shaw Robert B., 'Philip Larkin: A Stateside View', *Poetry Nation*, no. 6 (1976) 100–9.

Skelton, Robin, 'Comment' on *Oxford Book of Twentieth-Century English Verse*, in *Malahat Review*, no. 27 (July 1973) 5–7.

Spender, Stephen, review of *The Oxford Book of Twentieth-Century English Verse*, in *Spectator*, 31 Mar 1973, pp. 394–5.

——, *The Struggle of the Modern* (1963; repr. London: Methuen, 1965).

Swigg, Richard, 'Descending to the Commonplace', *PN Review*, 4, no. 2 (1977) 3–13.

Swinden, Patrick, 'Old Lines, New Lines: The Movement Ten Years After', *Critical Quarterly*, 9 (1967) 347–59.

——, review of *High Windows*, in *Critical Quarterly*, 16 (1974) 280–2.

Thurley, Geoffrey, *The Ironic Harvest: English Poetry in the Twentieth Century* (London: Edward Arnold, 1974).

Thwaite, Anthony, 'Larkin's Recent Uncollected Poems', *Phoenix*, nos 11–12 (Autumn–Winter 1973–4) 59–61.
——, 'The Poetry of Philip Larkin', in *The Survival of Poetry: A Contemporary Survey.* ed. Martin Dodsworth (London: Faber and Faber, 1970) pp. 37–55.
——, *Twentieth-Century English Poetry* (London: Heinemann, 1978).
Timms, David, ' "Church Going" Revisited: "The Building" and the Notion of Development', *Phoenix*, nos 11–12 (Autumn–Winter 1973–4) 13–25.
——, *Philip Larkin* (Edinburgh: Oliver and Boyd, 1973).
Tolley, A. T., 'Rhetoric and the Moderns', *Southern Review*, 6 (1970) 380–97.
Tomlinson, Charles, 'Poetry Today', in *The Pelican Guide to English Literature*, vol. VII: *The Modern Age*, ed. Boris Ford, 2nd edn (Harmondsworth: Penguin, 1963) pp. 458–74.
Wain, John, 'Art, if You Like', review of *All What Jazz*, in *Encounter*, 34 (May 1970) 68–71.
——, 'Engagement or Withdrawal? Some Notes on the Work of Philip Larkin', *Critical Quarterly*, 6 (1964) 167–78.
——, 'English Poetry: The Immediate Situation', *Sewanee Review*, 65 (1957) 353–74.
——, 'The Poetry of Philip Larkin', *Malahat Review*, no. 39 (July 1976) 95–112.
Ward, Geoffrey, 'Remembering the Movement', review of Blake Morrison, *The Movement*, in *Cambridge Quarterly*, 10 (1980) 67–75.
Watson, J. R., 'The Other Larkin', *Critical Quarterly*, 17 (1975) 347–61.
Weatherhead, A. Kingsley, 'Philip Larkin of England', *ELH*, 38 (1971) 616–30.
Whalen, Terry, ' "Being Serious and Being Funny": Philip Larkin's Irony and Sarcasm', *Thalia: Studies in Literary Humour*, 4, no. 2 (Fall–Winter 1981–2) 10–14.
——, 'Lawrence and Larkin: The Suggestion of an Affinity', *Modernist Studies*, 4 (1982) 105–22.
——, 'Many Larkins', review of Simon Petch, *The Art of Philip Larkin*, in *Australian Book Review*, no. 42 (July 1982) 35.
——, 'On Philip Larkin's Detachment', *Sift*, no. 1 (1973) 28–35.
——, 'Philip Larkin: Detachment or Impersonality?', *Critical Review*, no. 23 (1981) 20–33.
——, 'Philip Larkin's Imagist Bias: His Poetry of Observation', *Critical Quarterly*, 23, no. 2 (Summer 1981) 29–46.
Wood, Michael, 'Across the Irish Sea', review of Austin Clarke's *Collected Poems*, D. J. Enright's *The Terrible Shears*, and *High Windows*, *Parnassus*, 4, no. 1 (Fall–Winter 1975) 41–9.
——, 'We All Hate Home: English Poetry since World War II', *Contemporary Literature*, 18 (Summer 1977) 305–18.
Woodcock, George, 'Old and New Oxford Books: The Idea of An Anthology', review of *The Oxford Book of Twentieth-Century English Verse*, in *Sewanee Review*, 82 (1974) 119–30.

Index

160